THE WOMBLES

Elisabeth Beresford

Illustrated by Nick Price

GALAXY

PLUS

First published in Great Britain in 1968
by Ernest Benn Limited
This Large Print edition licensed and
published by AudioGO Ltd
by arrangement with
Bloomsbury Publishing Plc 2011

ISBN: 978 1405 664820

British Library Cataloguing in Publication Data available

Printed and bound in Great Britain by
CPI Antony Rowe, Chippenham and Eastbourne

CHAPTER 1

BUNGO

Once upon a time the Wombles went to live on—
or rather under—Wimbledon Common in South-
west London. There may be other Womble
families in different parts of the world—in fact,
there are—but the Wombles like to keep
themselves to themselves, so once they've made
a move and built themselves a comfortable
waterproof burrow they tend to stay where they
are.

The head of the Wimbledon Wombles is Great
Uncle Bulgaria. He is very old indeed and his fur
has turned snow-white and he feels the cold rather
badly. So during the winter months he mostly sits
in his own room in a large rocking chair, wearing a
tartan shawl and two pairs of spectacles. He uses
one pair for reading *The Times* newspaper and the
other for looking at young Wombles who have
misbehaved, and as this pair makes his eyes look

1

ENORMOUS it has a very alarming effect. Many a young Womble has come out of Great Uncle Bulgaria's room with his (or her) fur standing up on end and his (or her) teeth chattering.

As well as the rocking chair there is a footstool and an electric fire. Years and years ago when Great Uncle Bulgaria's fur was just turning from grey to white, he had a coal fire which gave a lot of trouble. If the wind was blowing a certain way his room used to get full of smoke which made him cough and, even worse, when the wind was not blowing at all the smoke went straight up the chimney and up through the bracken and the Common Keepers would go and stamp all over the ground thinking it was a fire in the bushes. And when they did that pieces of mud fell down the chimney into Great Uncle Bulgaria's room and made a dreadful mess and an even more dreadful smell. So Tobermory, who is very clever with his paws, made an electric fire out of bits of this and pieces of that and it makes the room nice and warm and gives no trouble at all.

And last, but very important indeed, there is Great Uncle Bulgaria's atlas. It is very large and very old and the pages have gone brown round the edges and some of them have come loose as well, although Tobermory has done his best to keep them in place with strips of sticky paper. It's a job which he dislikes because the sticky paper gets stuck to his fur, and the more he tries to get it off the more it sticks, so many of the maps have pieces of fur down the sides. The atlas is important because all the Wombles choose their own names out of it. Some of them spend a long, long time looking at all the different parts of the world to find just what will suit them, and some of them merely shut their eyes tight and point and hope for the best.

Which is how Bungo got *his* name.

'Serves you right,' said Great Uncle Bulgaria.

'I don't care, I like it,' said Bungo.

'Ho-hum,' said Great Uncle Bulgaria. 'Bungo it is then. Silly sort of name, but it quite suits *you*. Now then, young Womble, you're old enough to start work, which means you'll be going out on to the Common on your own. And *that* means you'll come across People, and People are very strange creatures.'

'I know,' said Bungo.

'No you don't. There's a lot you don't know. In fact, there's precious little you *do* know. Stand up straight and don't slouch. People are strange because they are untidy. Because they sometimes don't tell the truth and because most of them are so interested in their own affairs they just don't notice us. If possible you should avoid them, but if for one reason or another you have to speak to a Human Being always be polite and helpful. The chances are that they'll never even notice you're a Womble at all. But it's better to be safe than sorry so don't go looking for trouble. Now off you go and start work. *Bungo* indeed!'

And Great Uncle Bulgaria picked up *The Times* and shook out the pages and began to read, so Bungo went off feeling a little foolish, which was most unusual for him as he was quite certain that he was the bravest, the most adventurous and perhaps even the handsomest of all the Wombles.

He trotted down the long underground passage past all the small side turnings till he came to a

3

door with WORKSHOP painted on it.

'Come in, come in,' said Tobermory's gruff voice when Bungo knocked.

Bungo had never been in the Workshop before and he went in rather timidly and his small eyes grew large as he looked about him. It was a big room with rows and rows of shelves all round the walls and each shelf was stacked high with all kinds of things. Gloves, shoes, gumboots, scarves, cameras, balls, racquets, skates, fishing rods, sticks, handbags, wallets, sweaters, socks, jars, bottles, Thermos flasks, papers, books, watches, brooches, necklaces, hats, suitcases, raincoats, baskets, buckets, all kinds of money and a lot more besides. All of them in neat piles and each pile neatly labelled, for the Wombles are the tidiest creatures in the world.

And as if that wasn't enough to be going on with there were other rooms beyond with racks of larger objects. Bicycles and tricycles and scooters. Prams and deckchairs, wheels and tables and even parts of cars and caravans.

'Well!' said Bungo, slowly turning round and round.

'Ah ha!' said Tobermory, who was taking a radio to pieces on his workbench. His fur was turning grey and he wore a large blue apron and had a screwdriver tucked behind one ear and a pencil behind the other.

'Well, well, WELL,' said Bungo.

'What do you think of it, eh?' said Tobermory, his sharp eyes looking at Bungo although his busy paws never stopped working.

'It's very big, isn't it?' said Bungo. 'And there are such a lot of things. Do they all come from—?' and

4

he jerked his head towards the ceiling.

'That they do. All left by People out on the Common. Pass me that tin marked "screws", young Womble.'

'I've got a name now. I'm—' Bungo cleared his throat and looked rather shyly at Tobermory as he handed over the tin '—I'm Bungo. I *chose* it.'

'Sort of name you *would* choose. Silly sort of name. Yes, all my stores come from the Common. Human Beings are an untidy lot. They'd lose their legs and arms if they weren't joined on right. So you're old enough to start work, eh? Go and find yourself a basket. Over there, young Womble, on that shelf marked "Baskets". Can't you read?'

' 'Course I can,' said Bungo, rather hurt; but Tobermory was holding the radio up to his ear and shaking it and he didn't seem to hear, so Bungo sighed and went over to the shelf, where he picked out a large straw basket.

'Nice bit of work that,' said Tobermory, putting down the radio and looking at the basket. 'Hardly had to mend it at all when it was brought down to me. Just a stitch or two. Now remember, young Womble, it's our duty to keep the Common tidy. Just do your work properly and mind out for dogs. Dogs don't like Wombles and Wombles don't take kindly to dogs. Remember that. Now off you go! I'm busy.'

'*I'm* not afraid of dogs,' said Bungo.

'More fool you then,' said Tobermory. 'Shut the door behind you.'

Bungo had been looking forward to his first working day, for it's the point in a Womble's life when he feels nearly grown up. He has his own name at last and he is considered old enough and clever enough to venture into the outside world. In fact, Bungo had spent the last few nights imagining just how important he would feel and what a chance it would be to prove how brave and adventurous he was, but neither Great Uncle Bulgaria nor Tobermory had made any fuss of him, indeed they had called his spendid new name 'silly'.

'I'll show 'em,' muttered Bungo, doubling up his paws as he hurried down the passage. 'And if I meet any dogs I'll show *them* too.' And he gave a hop, skip and a jump because he suddenly felt excited again.

He pretended not to see all the other young Wombles whom he passed and his nose was very much in the air until he reached the main door which opened on to the Common. Sitting beside the door and reading a comic very slowly was the Nightwatch Womble, Tomsk. He blinked sleepily at Bungo, asked his name and wrote it down carefully in a large book. Then he unlocked the door and opened it and at once Bungo could smell the cool dawn air and hear the birds and a dog barking in the distance and all at once he didn't feel quite so brave after all.

However he couldn't let Tomsk know that, so Bungo whistled softly to himself and then hummed as the door was shut behind him and then very, very slowly he walked up the last winding passage until there was nothing between him and the outside world but bushes and ferns.

Bungo's nose appeared first and then his bright little eyes and then his round, furry body. As he was not very tall he couldn't see much except the tops of the bushes, which were laced with spiders'

webs and dew that glittered and danced in the early morning sunlight.

Bungo parted the bushes and edged his way between the leaves and grunted to himself as he made for the patch of Common which he was to look after. It was not a very large piece, but it had got a wooden bench on it and Bungo knew, from listening to the conversation of other Wombles, that where there was a seat for Human Beings there was also bound to be something to tidy up. He soon noticed some pieces of paper and within a few seconds Bungo's paws had picked up two chocolate bar wrappers, a handkerchief with 'D. Smith' on it, and an evening paper.

'*Tsk, tsk, tsk,*' said Bungo, feeling quite a Womble of the world, 'they're an untidy lot these Humans. *Tsk, tsk, tsk.*'

Once he started looking it was really astonishing how much there was to find. A pencil, one half of a return railway ticket to Victoria Station, quite a long piece of string and a library ticket were soon added to Bungo's collection, and he became so pleased with himself that he completely failed to notice two things: first, that the barking dog was getting closer all the time and second, that there was somebody sitting on the bench; until, just as he was about to seize a rather battered straw boater hat with both eager paws, a voice said almost in Bungo's horrified ear, 'And what do you think you're doing, may I ask?'

'*Eeeeep*,' said Bungo, diving under the seat and covering his ears with his paws.

'*That*,' said the voice, 'is *my* hat, I'll have you know.'

Bungo opened one eye and looked up, and into the eyes of somebody who was leaning right over the edge of the seat and looking down at him. Although the face was, of course, upside down, Bungo recognised it and his heart stopped making a loud banging noise and he said weakly, 'It was a joke.'

'*Poof!*'

'It was,' said Bungo, climbing out from under the seat and smoothing some of the grass off his fur. 'I knew it was your hat all the time, Orinoco.'

'*Poof*,' said Orinoco, who was the stoutest (and laziest) of all the Wimbledon Wombles. He sat back on the bench and put on the straw boater and tilted it over his eyes. He was also wearing sunglasses and a long overcoat—rather strained about the middle buttons—and at his side was a walking stick with a very pointed end and an extremely small paper carrier bag which was quite empty.

'I'm Bungo now,' said Bungo.

'I always like to sit in the sun,' said Orinoco,

taking no notice. 'A bit of sun does you a power of good. Hallo, there's a dog coming.'

'What shall we do?' asked Bungo, starting to tremble and quite forgetting that only a short while ago he had been so brave about dogs. But then he'd only seen a small one before now, and this dog was enormous with white fur and black spots and a long tongue.

'Do? I shan't *do* anything,' said Orinoco. 'I haven't had my forty winks yet.'

Bungo looked at Orinoco, who had folded his paws across his stomach and then at the dog, which was racing towards them, and one second later Bungo, that adventurous and fearless Womble, was running too. Across the grass he went with his ears back and his breath coming in great gasps until he reached the nearest tree and up that he clambered until he was lost among the golden yellow leaves.

The dog pranced and danced round the bottom and far up above Bungo shut his eyes and dug his claws into the wood and wished very hard indeed that he was just a young Womble again and safe deep inside the burrow.

'*Grrrrrr*,' said the Dalmatian, pawing at the tree trunk.

'Come here, Fred,' said the Dalmatian's owner, striding across the grass towards the bench where Orinoco was now gently snoring.

Much to Bungo's relief the Dalmatian shook its head and then reluctantly retreated to where its owner was about to sit down on the bench. Bungo parted the leaves and watched with his mouth open as he remembered Great Uncle Bulgaria's words of warning about mixing with Human Beings. There was a terrible story that once long,

long ago a Womble had been taken away by some men and had never been seen again. What had happened to him nobody knew and Bungo shivered so hard as he remembered this awful tale that the leaves shook gently.

'Lovely morning, sir,' said the man, sitting down and hanging on tightly to his dog's collar to stop it from sniffing round Orinoco's ankles.

'Zzzzzz,' said Orinoco sleepily. He was dreaming of breakfast and he scratched his stomach contentedly at the thought of food. The man moved away slightly, pulling his dog with him. The dog whined and showed his teeth and Bungo trembled so violently that some leaves drifted down off the tree.

'A very mild autumn we're having,' the man said.

'*Slup, slup, slup,*' said Orinoco, licking his lips as a picture of blackberries and cream slid before his eyes.

'Well, I must be getting along,' said the man rather nervously. '*Slup*' is a strange noise, especially when made by a stranger.

'*Oooof,*' said Orinoco, blowing out his cheeks and having a really good scratch.

'Nice meeting you,' the man said. 'Come along then, Fred,' and he caught hold of the Dalmatian's collar and pulled him away and went off very quickly without looking back. It wasn't until he was quite out of sight that Bungo slid down the tree and then, still feeling rather shaky, went over to Orinoco and nudged him.

'Whassat?' said Orinoco, sitting bolt upright. 'Oh, it's you again. What a restless creature you are. Isn't it breakfast time yet? Where's my hat?'

'On your head,' said Bungo. 'Weren't you

10

frightened of that man and his dog?'

'Man? What man? Dog? What dog?' said Orinoco, yawning. Then he took off his sunglasses and looked at Bungo and his eyes weren't at all sleepy as he added, 'When I've got these spectacles on there's a lot I don't see, although I'm not saying that I miss *much*. Such as young Wombles who run away from dogs . . .'

'But . . .' said Bungo, shuffling his paws.

'Or,' said Orinoco, picking up his stick, 'I might notice that my tidy-bag's rather empty while somebody else's basket seems quite full.'

'But . . .' said Bungo and then stopped and thought for a bit. And then he sighed and picked up his basket and began to take out some of the things and to put them in the bag.

'Nothing like a nice nap in the sun to make you feel fit,' said Orinoco, shutting his eyes again.

That evening Tobermory went along to have a goodnight chat with Great Uncle Bulgaria, who was just finishing the back page of *The Times*.

'Sit down, sit down,' said Great Uncle Bulgaria, pushing over the stool. Tobermory sat down and spread out his paws to the electric fire.

'Nothing to read in the paper these days,' said Great Uncle Bulgaria, hitching his tartan shawl more firmly round his shoulders. 'Well, how's young Bungo—silly name that—how's he coming along?'

'He'll do,' said Tobermory and smiled to himself behind his paw. 'Thinks he's the greatest Womble in the world at the moment, but he'll soon get *that* knocked out of him. One way and another.'

'He's young yet,' said Great Uncle Bulgaria and for a moment the two wise old Wombles looked at

11

each other and then Great Uncle Bulgaria got out the chess game which he and Tobermory had been playing for years and years and quite soon both of them had forgotten all about Bungo.

And as for Bungo himself, he was fast asleep with a happy smile on his face, for he was dreaming that he was chasing an enormous black and white Dalmatian clean across Wimbledon Common while all the other Wombles watched him admiringly . . .

CHAPTER 2

ORINOCO AND THE BLACK UMBRELLA

'Good morning,' said Bungo, putting his nose round the Workshop door.

'You're late,' said Tobermory, looking at the shelf which held the clocks and watches. As he had got most of them in working order and wound up they made a busy ticking noise, like dozens of pecking birds.

'I overslept,' said Bungo.

He hadn't got used to being a working Womble yet and in the evenings he was often so tired that he couldn't keep his eyes open and he would nod off with his head on another Womble's shoulder, lulled by the steady rumble of voices; for if there is one thing that Wombles are really fond of it's the sound of their own voices. And there was a great deal to discuss at the moment with Christmas only two months away and after that the planning of the Great Womble Outing. Midsummer's Eve is the

13

most important night of the year as far as the Wimbledon Wombles are concerned. They have a tremendous party and it takes a great deal of organising. So it just goes to show how tired Bungo must have been to go to sleep while all *that* was being discussed.

Perhaps Tobermory understood, for after a quick glance at Bungo he only said, '*Tsk, tsk, tsk.* Well off you go then, and remember to keep your back paws firmly on the ground.'

'Why?' asked Bungo.

'Wait and see,' said Tobermory, and began putting a camera together on his workbench, his paws neatly and carefully picking up each tiny screw, and examining it through a jeweller's glass which he had fixed into his eye.

It didn't take Bungo long to discover what Tobermory had meant, for the moment the main door of the burrow was opened he was nearly blown backwards by the wind. Small dry leaves and dust and tiny scraps of paper whirled past his head and his fur was quite flattened.

'Whoops,' said Bungo, dragging the door shut behind him and leaning against it. He had never been out in a gale before as a high wind is dangerous to small Wombles and can blow them clean off their paws. Bungo turned his back on it and felt his eyes watering as he worked his way through the bushes, while all the time twigs and leaves were rattling about his head and the trees up above were bending and creaking and throwing their branches about.

'Thought you were never coming,' said Orinoco, who had made himself a comfortable nest in among the bushes. 'Well, there's a lot of work to be

14

done.'

And there was, for the wind had driven across the streets and gardens of South-west London before it reached the Common and on its journey it had picked up everything in its path. There were newspapers and paper bags, handkerchiefs and hats, scarves and gloves, bus tickets and shopping lists and notes left for milkmen, and a lot more besides, all scudding happily across the grass and through the bushes.

Orinoco had already found a scarf (red and white stripes), and had wrapped it round and round his neck and then over his straw hat to keep it in place.

'We'll never tidy up all this,' said Bungo in dismay.

'Got to try,' said Orinoco. 'I've made a start.' And he twitched at the scarf. 'Now off you go, young Bungo, while I get my breath back.' And he settled down and shut his eyes.

For the next hour Bungo trotted backwards and forwards chasing the papers and stuffing them into his shopping basket. But as soon as he had cleared one patch of Common the wind sent another shoal of bits and pieces dancing through the air. In spite of the cold—it was a north wind—Bungo was soon very warm indeed, so he wedged his basket firmly between two tree stumps and went puffing and panting down to Queen's Mere to have a drink of water.

There was nobody about apart from the ducks and Bungo stopped to watch them riding on the water, which was quite choppy and full of leaves. He was just thinking about going back to work when he noticed something long and black caught in the rushes, and although the pond was not one of the places which he had to keep tidy, being Bungo he couldn't resist going to have a closer look, so he slid into the water and swam across.

'It's a stick with stuff on it,' said Bungo, circling round the thing. One of the ducks came quacking over and Bungo slapped the water with his paws and the duck sailed away again.

'Silly thing,' said Bungo, who like most Wombles didn't think much of ducks, rabbits and squirrels. He got hold of the long black thing between his teeth and pulled it free and began to swim back to the shore rather slowly, for the object was large and awkward. Once on firm ground Bungo put it down and shook himself thoroughly, and then put the thing under his arm, collected his shopping basket and hurried off to Orinoco.

Orinoco was sound asleep, but he woke up at once when he heard Bungo and sat up and pretended to be very busy looking through the three bus tickets in his tidy-bag.

'Look what I've found,' said Bungo, laying the thing at Orinoco's paws.

'That's nothing to get excited about—it's only an old umbrella,' said Orinoco.

Now Bungo was a good-hearted Womble who would never do anyone a bad turn, but it did occur to him at this moment that it was rather unfair that he should work so hard while Orinoco hardly did a paw's turn. Perhaps it was because Orinoco was being so squashing about the umbrella.

'It's a very splendid umbrella,' Bungo said. He had actually never seen one before because he hadn't yet been all round the Workshop, where, as it happened, Tobermory had a very good selection

of umbrellas and even a couple of parasol
And he picked it up and twirled it rc
round his head in exactly the same way
Uncle Bulgaria twirled his stick sometimes

'That's not the way to use it,' said Orinoco, and
he got up out of his nest and took the umbrella
from Bungo's paws and opened it up. Now
although Orinoco was quite fat (no Womble is
what you might call *thin*, but Orinoco was fatter
than most), the wind was exceptionally strong, and
the umbrella particularly large, and before
Orinoco or Bungo knew quite what was happening
Orinoco was being swept over the grass as fast as
his short back legs would carry him.

'Hang on, hang on,' said Bungo, dancing up and
down.

'I am hanging on,' Orinoco shouted back, for a
Womble, once it's attached to something, simply
will *not* let go.

He was on the top of a high ridge of ground by
this time and suddenly the wind lifted him clean
off his paws and took him straight up towards the
sky.

'Come back,' shouted Bungo.

'I can't,' shouted Orinoco.

Up and up he went, peering over his shoulder at
the ground, which was now spreading out beneath
him so that he could see the tops of the tossing
trees and the ruffled water of Queen's Mere. And
beyond that there was the Windmill and the Golf
Course and beyond *that* the road to one side of the
Common with the early morning rush-hour traffic
just starting to build up. He could even see the
roofs of the houses and a building site where the
workmen were coming on duty. He only needed to

a little bit higher and he might have been able o see the dome of St Paul's far away to the east.

Orinoco gave a dreadful groan and gripped the umbrella handle harder than ever. Because of his fatness he had stopped climbing trees some time ago and he had rather lost his head for heights, and in any case this was a great deal higher than any Womble had ever been before. If he could have gone green with fright and airsickness Orinoco would have done so, but as it was all he could do was to groan.

Far, far below Bungo was nearly as worried as Orinoco. Supposing he was blown right over London? Supposing he hit some tall trees or a building or got caught in some wires? Supposing he was never seen again? All kinds of dreadful ideas went through Bungo's mind as he ran puffing and panting over the grass trying to keep up with Orinoco's progress through the sky.

It was the umbrella, which had started all the trouble, that put an end to the awful journey. It had never been made to be blown through the air with a fat Womble hanging on to it, and quite suddenly there was a horrible creaking sound above Orinoco's head and as he looked up he saw the umbrella shiver and shake and then there was a ripping noise and all the spokes rushed upwards and the umbrella turned itself inside out. It was Orinoco's good fortune that it chose to do this just as they scudded over Queen's Mere.

'*Yow!*' yelled Orinoco.

The air rushed past him, flattening his fur, and he began to fall faster and faster until there was a whistling sound in his ears.

'*Yooow!*' roared Orinoco and shut his eyes and

the next moment he hit the lake with a tremendous smack, sending up a great shower of water and making every duck swim for cover as hard as it could go. Down and down went Orinoco right to the muddy bottom, and then with his head whirling and his mouth—which had been open at the time—full of weeds he rose slowly to the surface, the umbrella still tightly grasped between his paws.

'I'm coming,' panted Bungo, sliding and slipping down the steep bank, and he dived into the Mere for the second time that morning.

Orinoco rolled over on to his back and lay quite still with his eyes closed, his paws crossed over his stomach, the umbrella held between them.

'I've got you,' puffed Bungo, fighting his way through the ripples, for Orinoco's fall had set up a widening circle of tidal waves which were now splashing on to the ground. And he put his paws over Orinoco's ears and began to pull him towards dry land, paddling as hard as he could go. Orinoco, as stiff as a poker, was hauled wet and extremely muddy on to the path.

'Are you dead?' Bungo asked anxiously.

'Yes,' said Orinoco in a feeble voice, without opening his eyes.

'Oh dear,' said Bungo.

'Very, very nearly dead anyway,' said Orinoco, opening one eye a little. 'What are you laughing at? Being nearly dead is not at all funny.'

'No, rather not,' said Bungo, snuffling behind his paw.

'When I think of what I've been through,' said Orinoco, opening the other eye and looking sternly at the quivering Bungo, 'I expect sympathy, not giggling. If you only knew what it was like!' And he shivered violently.

'I'm sorry, truly I am,' said Bungo, putting both paws over his mouth. 'But all the same, Orinoco, if *you* only knew what you look like with weeds in your fur—and your hat's gone very p-peculiar.'

'My hat?' said Orinoco weakly, and sat up.

Instead of a boater he was now wearing what looked like a bonnet, for the straw had gone all soggy and, what with that, and the mud and the weeds and the relief, Bungo could contain himself no longer and he flopped down on the ground and laughed until his stomach ached and the tears squeezed out of his eyes.

'If you only knew what you l-looked like,' Bungo said wheezily. 'Flying through the air and groaning and moaning and then zip, bang, crash, wallop, down into the water and then bubble, bubble, slosh, bosh, up again and now—ho, ho, ho, HO!'

'I don't think it's at all *funny*,' said Orinoco coldly. 'Not funny in the least little tiny bit.'

'No, oh no, rather NOT,' said Bungo, flapping his paws feebly. 'Not funny at all really. HO, HO, HO, HO!'

Orinoco rose with great dignity and went down to the water's edge and took off his scarf and wrung it out, and then he shook his hat, which would never be the same again, and then he cleaned his fur and shook himself. And finally he picked up the umbrella and still without a word and with his nose in the air he led the way back to their patch of Common, with Bungo still snorting and sniffing, trotting along behind him.

At last Orinoco spoke.

'I'm worn out,' he said. 'Abso-lutely ex-haus-ted. What I need is a good forty winks.' And he began to flatten out his little nest in the bushes. Bungo looked at him and then at the umbrella, and then at Orinoco's very nearly empty tidy-bag and finally at the patch which they were supposed to keep tidy, and which was now covered again with newspapers and bus tickets and even some rusty old tins.

'No, you don't,' said Bungo daringly. 'What you need is something to warm you up. Like work.'

Orinoco stopped nest-making and looked at Bungo over his shoulder.

'Dalmatian dogs,' Orinoco said.

'Black umbrellas, zip, bang, crash, wallop,' said Bungo.

There was a long silence, which was only broken by the roar of the wind and the rattling of the trees and then very, very slowly Orinoco straightened up and shook his head sadly.

'All right, young Bungo. Very well. But just this once, that's all.'

When Tobermory saw the umbrella he shook his head over it, said '*Tsk, tsk, tsk*', and put it on the end of his workbench to be mended later.

'Haven't got time to attend to it at the moment,' he said. 'It's been a very busy day.'

And indeed the usually neat Workshop had mounds and mounds of things all over the floor, and a number of Wombles were hard at work sorting through the piles.

'I hope you managed to keep your paws on the ground all right,' said Tobermory as Bungo reached the door.

'Oh rather,' said Bungo, '*I* didn't have any trouble at all.' And he went off whistling and with such a wide smile on his face that Tobermory spent

21

at least ten seconds scratching his head and wondering what he had been up to. And as Bungo was, after all, a very good-hearted Womble he never mentioned the umbrella to Orinoco again. Unfortunately Orinoco was not cured of his laziness; it would take much more than an air trip across the Common to do *that*. And as for the umbrella itself—well, once Tobermory had mended it and cleaned it he decided to . . .

But that's another story altogether.

CHAPTER 3

THE TREE THAT MOVED

The terrible wind died down almost as suddenly as it had started, and for half an hour or so the Common was quiet and hushed, and the roar and rumble of the traffic on the roads could be heard quite clearly. The trees stood still as statues and every creature small and large let out a sigh of relief and began to get its breath back. Even the youngest Wombles, who were fast asleep, stirred and muttered and turned over, for the noise of the wind had been heard deep down in the burrow and for a week doors had banged and the electric lights had swung backwards and forwards, making leaping shadows on the walls.

But now it was quiet. So quiet that Great Uncle Bulgaria, who had been making out the Midsummer party timetable with Tobermory, put down his pencil and listened with his head cocked on one side.

'Wind's dropped,' said Great Uncle Bulgaria.

'Good thing too,' grunted Tobermory, who was tired out. Of all the Wombles he was the tidiest and it irritated him to see his precious Workshop piled high with all the things which had been collected from the Common. There just hadn't been time to get everything sorted out, and for the last two nights he had been dreaming about being overtaken by an avalanche of hats and scarves, papers and boxes, bus tickets and milk cartons. Even the smallest Wombles had been made to help with the clearing and sorting out, and although they did their best they weren't properly trained and they *would* get underneath Tobermory's paws.

'Worst wind I remember,' said Tobermory, rubbing his eyes. His fur felt sticky with tiredness.

'Ho-hum,' said Great Uncle Bulgaria, whose memory went further back than his friend's and who could recall the Great Storm, which had blown down dozens of trees. 'Well, time you went to bed.'

'What about you?' said Tobermory, putting his paw over his mouth to hide a yawn.

'You don't need much sleep when you get to my age,' said Great Uncle Bulgaria. 'Besides . . . well, never mind. Off you go, old friend, and no more nightmares.'

Great Uncle Bulgaria drew his tartan shawl more closely about his shoulders and put his paws up on the footstool and blinked at the electric fire. He didn't like sudden silences. A stillness in the air was all right on a lovely summer's evening or a spring night, but in November it didn't feel right, and Great Uncle Bulgaria could sense his fur prickling, which was always a sign of something

24

being not as it should be.

'Ha-ho-hum,' muttered Great Uncle Bulgaria, and he got up very slowly and felt for his stick and then shuffled quietly out of his warm room and down the passages, where the only sound was the gentle breathing of the sleeping Wombles and the ticking of the clocks in the Workshop.

The lights were turned down low and the old Womble's shadow was pale grey as it now kept up with him, then leapt ahead, and then fell behind as he passed each small beacon of light.

In spite of his age Great Uncle Bulgaria moved so softly that he almost surprised the Womble who was on duty at the main doorway. Luckily for the Nightwatch Womble, Great Uncle Bulgaria just happened to drop his stick.

'What? Who? Which?' said the Womble, leaping to his paws.

'It's me,' said Great Uncle Bulgaria, shuffling round the corner, and peering through his spectacles. 'Who's that?'

'Tomsk,' said the Womble.

He was twice the size of Great Uncle Bulgaria, indeed he was the largest Womble on the Common. He was also the bravest and the most daring for he would climb the highest tree or dive to the bottom of Queen's Mere, and he had once chased after an Alsatian. Fortunately he had not caught it, for he would not have had the least idea what to have done with it. For the truth of the matter was that Tomsk had no common sense at all.

He had nearly driven Tobermory demented on the one occasion when he had been sent to help in the Workshop, for he had put everything away in

25

the wrong place. He was not much good at tidying up either, for he ambled about in his slow, deliberate way, completely forgetting to keep clear of dogs and Human Beings. So now he was working as a Nightwatch Womble where even he could hardly make any mistakes. But it was rather a lonely job, so he was quite glad to have someone to talk to, even if that someone was Great Uncle Bulgaria, who could be very fierce.

'Asleep?' growled Great Uncle Bulgaria, prodding Tomsk with his stick.

'Yes,' said Tomsk, hanging his head and twisting one paw round another. A Womble can never, under any circumstances, tell a lie. [To call another Womble 'a liar' is the worst of all insults.]

'Should be ashamed of yourself,' said Great Uncle Bulgaria. 'Womble safety depends on you. Well, don't do it again and open up.'

'*Now?*' said Tomsk. 'Open up *now*? It's the middle of the night.'

'I know it's the middle of the night,' said Great Uncle Bulgaria. 'Go on. Go on.'

Tomsk shook his head and slid back the bolts very slowly and then opened the door a few inches.

'More than that,' said Great Uncle Bulgaria. 'I want to go OUT.'

'*Now?*' said Tomsk.

At which Great Uncle Bulgaria blew out his cheeks and hooked the door open with his stick and shuffled out into the cold, still air. He was glad of his shawl as he made his way through the bushes and out into the dark night. He saw the white and black face of a badger watching him from the shadows and muttered, ' 'Evening.'

The badger, which like the Wombles had been

26

disturbed by the sudden silence, grunted deep in its throat and ambled back into the darkness. A couple of rats squeaked and for a second their eyes shone in the starlight and then they too were gone.

Great Uncle Bulgaria looked up at the sky and saw that the stars were vanishing one by one as the clouds came rolling in from the west. He sniffed the air, turning his head from side to side and again his fur prickled for he could smell rain coming. Not just a shower, or even a good soaking, but a real downpour. There were thousands of gallons of water up in that clouding sky and Great Uncle Bulgaria didn't care for the smell of it at all.

'Anything the matter?' whispered Tomsk, looming up behind him.

'Going to rain,' said Great Uncle Bulgaria, and pattered back towards the burrow, leaving Tomsk more puzzled than ever.

As always Great Uncle Bulgaria was perfectly correct. The rain started with a soft sighing sound at ten minutes past two. As the night wore on the rain grew heavier and heavier and when the first Wombles stirred just before dawn it was coming down in steady driving sheets which were so thick you could hardly see through them.

'It's raining,' announced Tomsk as Bungo came bouncing jauntily down the passage.

'How can you tell?' said Bungo cheekily.

'Because I've seen it,' said Tomsk, 'and it was wet.'

'Oh, you *are* clever,' said Bungo very rudely indeed, and went to get his basket from the Workshop. Tobermory issued him with a pair of gumboots, an oilskin, and a sou'wester as well.

'I don't mind a drop of rain,' said Bungo.

27

'This isn't a drop, it's a flood,' said Tobermory. 'Don't argue.'

He had slept quite well, but he still wasn't in the best of tempers. Bungo made a face to himself and put on his rainclothes and went clumping off to the main door. He thought it was all a lot of fuss about nothing until he got outside, and then he blinked and choked because it was exactly like stepping into a waterfall. The rain plopped on to his hat and ran down the brim and fell on to his collar and slid down his coat and pattered on to his boots. It turned the grass into mud under his paws and it turned all the bits of paper into a horrid, pulpy mess as he tried to pick them up.

But the rain did much more than that, for it loosened the earth round the roots of the trees and gently but firmly swept it away in little rivers of mud. And the mud ran down the banks and the little rivers grew larger and they bit deeper and deeper into the ground until they made narrow valleys and everything got swept along before them. Sticks and stones and old leaves and bits of rubbish, they went tumbling downwards, leaving behind them uncovered roots which had nothing on which to take a grip. And at the same time the water in Queen's Mere began to rise; little by little and inch by inch it rose, until it lapped over on to the paths and met and mingled with the muddy streams coming down their sides.

'It's raining,' announced Bungo when he finally straggled back to the the burrow.

'Told you so,' said Tomsk. 'You do look wet.'

'I *am* wet,' said Bungo, taking off his rainclothes and shaking himself violently. 'Give us a paw with these boots.'

28

Tomsk took a good grip on them and pulled, and because he was so strong the boots came off at once, and Tomsk went staggering backwards and sat down with a thump which made his teeth rattle.

'Thanks,' said Bungo, and went off whistling, without even bothering to find out if Tomsk was hurt. Like a great many other Wombles Bungo didn't bother much about Tomsk, so Tomsk just sat still for a moment feeling rather sad for some reason. And it was while he was sitting that he noticed that a few leaves and bits of stick by the doorway were moving.

'That's funny,' said Tomsk, sitting on the ground with the boots in his lap. 'That's *very* funny.'

'What is?' asked Orinoco, coming in and stepping over Tomsk and shaking himself just as Bungo had done.

'The ground's moving,' said Tomsk. 'It's wobbling like a jelly.'

'Jelly?' said Orinoco, brightening up. 'Jelly, did you say? I hope it's blackberry jelly, because that's one of my favourites. Hang up my coat for me, will you? I've had a very hard morning.'

And off went Orinoco with six wet bus tickets in the bottom of his tidy-bag, and the firm belief in his head that he had been working every minute of the last three hours, instead of trying to find somewhere to shelter and have a nice forty winks.

'It *is* moving,' said Tomsk, who once he had got hold of an idea stuck to it very firmly. But all the other Wombles were too busy about their own affairs to take any notice of him, so Tomsk put the boots in a nice neat line and hung up the raincoats and hats, and then went back to watch the leaves and twigs creeping down the track towards the

29

main door. It was really quite a frightening thing to see, but Tomsk was not a nervous Womble so his fur didn't prickle as Great Uncle Bulgaria's would have done if he had been there.

The small tide of mud lapped over the doorstep and when Tomsk put his paw there the mud just went round the sides of it. Tomsk didn't care for the feeling very much and after thinking about it he decided to go and get a broom from the Workshop.

'What do you want?' growled Tobermory, whose fur was now covered with so many mushy pieces of white paper that he looked as if he had been making pastry.

'A broom,' said Tomsk.

'*You* don't need a broom,' said Tobermory. 'There now, you've made me lose count of these dratted baskets *and* you've left dirty pawmarks right across my floor.'

'It's only one paw that's dirty,' said Tomsk,

holding it up to show Tobermory. 'And I want a broom to stop the ground moving.'

'Don't come here with your nonsense,' said Tobermory, seizing Tomsk by the shoulders and pushing him towards the door. 'The ground doesn't move unless it's an earthquake, you silly great gormless Womble.'

'But . . .' said Tomsk.

However the door had been firmly shut in his face, so Tomsk gave an enormous sigh and went back to his post only to discover that his neat row of boots had all been pushed out of line by the moving mud. And, what was more, the hooks on which he had hung the dripping raincoats were all bulging out from the wall. Tomsk put one of his large paws against the wall and a crack appeared and ran right from the ceiling to the floor.

'It wasn't my fault,' said Tomsk, but there was no one round about to hear him, and Tomsk shifted from paw to paw wondering what on earth to do next. He knew he wasn't very clever, and everyone had told him that the ground couldn't move (except in an earthquake), but on the other hand even as he watched it the floor under his feet seemed to shimmer and shake and very slowly and gently Tomsk started to sink. It was such a nasty feeling that Tomsk decided there and then that he had better do something about it. If he couldn't get hold of a broom then a piece of brushwood would be the next best thing. He knew he wasn't supposed to desert his post until it was meal time, but the mud sliding down the passage was more important than anything else.

Tomsk put on the nearest hat and edged round the door and out into the driving rain. He had nearly to close his eyes to see properly, and each time he touched a branch or a bush he got another showerbath, but he only shook himself and went on searching for a nice large piece of brushwood. His paws had just closed on a sturdy branch when, as well as the steady roar of the rain, Tomsk heard something else. It was a sound that he had never heard before, even on this day of surprises, and although he was so wet it made his fur stand up in little prickly bunches. It was a deep and terrible sigh.

Tomsk put back his head and looked up, and there above him was a tall, thin tree which was moving too. Not one breath of wind was there and yet, although he had to keep blinking to keep the rain out of his eyes, Tomsk could see that the tree was slowly, but deliberately bending over.

'Stop, don't do that,' shouted Tomsk.

The tree sighed and shivered and creaked and two squirrels ran along its topmost branches and leapt for the safety of a nearby neighbour.

'Don't, don't, don't!' implored Tomsk, jumping up and down and banging his paws together.

'*Whooooo,*' sighed the tree and leant over even further. Tomsk looked round in a distracted fashion but there wasn't another Womble in sight, so without stopping to think any more, Tomsk launched himself through the brambles and the bushes and wrapped his strong arms round the trunk of the tree, scrabbling with his back paws to get a firm grip on the muddy ground.

'Help,' shouted Tomsk through the roar of the rain. 'Help! Wombles! Help!'

But there was no answer except from the tree, which sighed yet again, and despite Tomsk's

32

enormous efforts began to tilt slowly towards the roof of the Womble burrow. Tomsk dug his paws still deeper into the mud, closed his eyes and hung on with all his strength.

CHAPTER 4

TOMSK HANGS ON

'I thought Tomsk said it was jelly today,' said Orinoco, wiping his mouth and pushing back his chair with a contented sigh. 'But chocolate pudding is even nicer. I don't believe I could eat another mouthful.'

'You've had three helpings already,' said Bungo.

'I need it to keep up my strength,' said Orinoco. 'I've been working so hard.'

'That's what I like to hear,' said Tobermory, who was just walking past. 'A Womble who's keen to work hard.'

'Oh, I *am*,' said Orinoco. 'In fact, I did such a lot this morning that I thought I'd just go and have forty . . .'

'A Womble who's keen,' said Tobermory, taking hold of Orinoco's arm and propelling him towards the door, 'should never be discouraged. You can come and help me clear up in the Workshop. And what are you laughing at, young Bungo?'

'Nothing,' said Bungo, trying to make his mouth go into a straight line.

'I'm glad to hear it,' said Tobermory in such a quiet, gentle voice that Bungo forgot all about laughing and felt very solemn instead. 'You can come too. Two pairs of paws are better than one. *Brrr* . . . it's chilly out here.'

And it was, for Tomsk had left the main door open and now it couldn't have shut even if it had wanted to, for the mud had wedged it into position and the cold November air was drifting down the passages and into the rooms. A chilly breath of it even slid under Great Uncle Bulgaria's door and blew round his paws.

'Getting old,' muttered Great Uncle Bulgaria to himself, and drew his tartan shawl even closer and dozed off, lulled by the distant pattering of the rain.

Tobermory, still holding very firmly to the scruffs of Bungo and Orinoco, walked them to the Workshop and then gave them a final shake and pointed to a small side store where all that morning's papers had been piled in one soggy mass.

'You can clear that up for a start,' he said, and went off to put on his big blue apron to attend to more important matters such as some of the lights which had most mysteriously gone out.

'If you hadn't laughed . . .' muttered Orinoco.

'If you hadn't talked about working so hard . . .' replied Bungo.

The two Wombles glared at each other, and then began to pick up pawfuls of the horrid sludgy stuff and put it into buckets. Perhaps it was because there was a slight feeling of uneasiness in the air, or perhaps it was that they were both rather bad-tempered, but whatever it was one of them suddenly got the idea that it would be rather funny just to throw a little of the wet paper at the other. This particular Womble did it while the other Womble had his back to him, and it caught him just behind the ear with a wonderful squelching sound. So naturally the Womble who had been hit had to return the compliment, and in no time at all soggy pawfuls of wet and muddy paper were flying backwards and forwards like snowballs.

'Got you,' squealed Orinoco, catching Bungo straight between the eyes. Bungo shook his head and plunged both paws into the pile, and hit Orinoco with a left and a right. Orinoco staggered back against the wall and knocked over a bucket. With a speed which was surprising in one so fat he bent down and picked up the whole bucketload and threw that at Bungo. It plopped about his ears and ran down his head and into his eyes and his ears and his nose and even his mouth.

There was only one thing to do and Bungo did it. He picked up a bucket and aimed its contents at Orinoco, who was doubled up with laughter.

'Slosh!' The bucket of wet paper and mud sailed across the little storeroom just as Tobermory came through the doorway with a box of electric light bulbs, to see what all the noise was about. The wet, sticky, sloppy stuff caught him fair and square, and Tobermory let out a bellow which made the whole room shake.

Orinoco and Bungo moved as one. They leapt towards the door with their heads down, but

36

Tobermory was too quick for them. He dropped the bulbs, caught hold of the Wombles as they raced past him, and slapped their heads together so that for a moment all they could see were coloured lights going round and round.

'WHAT IS THE MEANING OF THIS?' roared Tobermory, shaking them so that their mouths flew open and then rattled shut.

'Wha' wha' wha' . . .' said Bungo.

'Woo woo woo . . .' said Orinoco.

'WHO STARTED IT?' bellowed Tobermory, whose fur—those bits of it which were not plastered with white, sticky mush—was trying to stand up on end with rage.

Bungo and Orinoco clamped their mouths shut and looked at each other through the coloured lights which were now growing fainter, although their heads were still ringing.

'Well?' said Tobermory, more quietly.

Although he was quite old he was still very strong, and he lifted both Wombles clean off the ground so that their paws were kicking and struggling in mid-air. He gave them another shake and both of them closed their eyes and hunched their shoulders up to their ears.

'If you won't tell me,' said Tobermory, kicking one of the buckets out of the way, 'I shall have to take you to Great Uncle Bulgaria, and as it's his time for a nap he will not be in the best of tempers.'

Still neither Womble spoke, so Tobermory turned on his heel and with Bungo and Orinoco held at arm's length he marched down the passage. As all three of them looked very strange, every other Womble that they passed stood still and stared and whispered.

Tobermory knocked on Great Uncle Bulgaria's door with his knee.

'Come in,' said a rather sleepy voice and then, when Great Uncle Bulgaria turned round and saw them he added, 'Bless me. What in the world does this mean?'

'You may well ask,' said Tobermory, giving them another shake before letting them down to the ground. 'My workshop looks more like a battlefield than anything else.'

'Ho-hum,' said Great Uncle Bulgaria, taking off one pair of spectacles and carefully replacing them with the pair which made his eyes seem twice as huge as normal. 'And shut that door, there's a good Womble. There's a dreadful draught in here and . . .'

Even as he spoke there was a distant rumbling sound and the lights flickered and went low and the electric fire sparked angrily to itself.

'What's that?' whispered Bungo, and so strange is Womble nature that he forgot he was frightened of Tobermory and moved closer to him for protection.

'Earthquake?' Tobermory said in a low voice, looking at Great Uncle Bulgaria, who had gone very still. And Tobermory forgot in his turn to be furious with Bungo, and patted his shoulder where the soggy paper and mud had begun to dry and turn hard.

'No,' said Great Uncle Bulgaria, his old head on one side, his ears cocked. 'It's—yes—I think it's a landslide.'

'Tomsk said the ground was moving this morning,' said Bungo in a rather shaky voice.

'Yes, he told me that too,' put in Orinoco.

'He happened to mention it to me as well,' added Tobermory.

Great Uncle Bulgaria pushed his stool away so violently that it toppled over.

'And why did nobody mention it to *me*?' he demanded. The three Wombles didn't reply, and Great Uncle Bulgaria shook his head and got to his paws, pulling his shawl round him.

'I'll deal with whatever all this is about later,' he said. 'At the moment the landslide is far more important. Go and find Tomsk and bring him here immediately. Do you understand?'

Bungo and Orinoco bundled out of the room, too scared at this new turn of events to feel relieved that they had escaped a lecture and punishment, at least for the moment. They scurried and ran from room to room looking for Tomsk and in every place they found little huddles of scared, whispering Wombles. But of Tomsk there was no sign although they did discover the half open door and the boots, which were now all jumbled together with the raincoats, which had fallen off the wall and become mixed up with pieces of earth and mud. The rain was still thundering down, and they were in too much of a panic to hear a very faint, exhausted voice out in the gathering darkness which was saying 'Help. Wombles. Help. Wombles' over and over again.

'No sign of him?' said Great Uncle Bulgaria, thumping the ground with his stick. 'This is ridiculous. Tomsk is not the sort of Womble to run away, even though there are others who are not particularly kind to him.' This was uttered with a sharp look at Bungo and Orinoco, who swallowed and fidgeted with their paws. Tobermory too looked rather uncomfortable and Great Uncle Bulgaria, who saw a great deal more than a lot of Wombles realised, said, '*Tsk, tsk, tsk*', and got his own waterproof and boots and an enormous sou'wester and put them on, and led the way down the passage where the lights were now extremely dim.

'Could be dangerous,' said Tobermory. 'I'd better switch them off altogether. Wombles,' he raised his voice, 'there's no cause for alarm, but you'd better light your emergency candles.'

Within minutes all the passages and rooms were plunged into darkness and then little stars of light began to appear, and at every doorway there were groups of Wombles with wide, scared eyes. Whispers flew up and down the burrow, but everybody remained calm as Great Uncle Bulgaria, carrying a storm lantern, led the way to the main door.

He held the lamp up high and Tobermory, Bungo and Orinoco picked their paws up so as not to trip over the boots and the coats and the slow-moving tide of rubbish. It was nearly dark outside by this time, and the rain looked like moving sheets of glass arrows as Great Uncle Bulgaria, helped by the others, pushed the door wide.

'Tomsk!' shouted Great Uncle Bulgaria.

'The walls, the burrow,' muttered Tobermory, who had noticed the bulges and cracks.

'A Womble is more important than wood and plaster,' Great Uncle Bulgaria said sternly.

'Sorry, I was forgetting,' said Tobermory. 'Right, all together, one, two, three, TOMSK!'

'Tomsk! Tomsk! TOMSK!' The shout echoed

through the dripping bushes and round the wet trees, drowning even the persistent hammering of the rain. And Tomsk, who had long ago forgotten almost who he was or what was happening, and who only knew that the most important thing was to hang on to the creaking, sighing tree, stirred and opened his tired eyes.

'Tomsk! Tomsk! TOMSK!' came the shout again, and Tomsk cleared his throat and shouted back as best he could in a cracked, thin voice.

'I'm here.'

He moved as he said it, and his grasp slackened, and the tree gave another of its awful deep groaning sighs, and this time the ground was too muddy for Tomsk's paws to grip any longer and although he hung on with all his strength it was of no use. For the tree had moved just that inch too much and now its power was greater than that of Tomsk. But of course a Womble, however exhausted he may be, just will not leave go, so Tomsk clung on, and as Great Uncle Bulgaria lifted up the storm lantern against the sheets of rain, the four Wombles in the doorway saw Tomsk slowly rise against the darkness of the black wet sky.

'Let go,' shouted Great Uncle Bulgaria.

But Tomsk's muscles had been gripping that tree for so long that they just could not relax. Tobermory, closely followed by Bungo and Orinoco, lunged through the sopping bushes, but they were too late. For one moment it seemed as if they would just grasp Tomsk's dangling paws and then with the most tremendous crash the tree toppled sideways and its roots shot up into the air and Tomsk went with them.

41

Mud and leaves, twigs and bushes, flew in all directions and there was a great deal of noise and then silence except for the rain.

'Tomsk,' called Great Uncle Bulgaria, and if there was a slight shake in his voice nobody but he noticed it.

'Up here,' called Tomsk huskily, and as Great Uncle Bulgaria raised the lantern they could just make out the dark shadow of Tomsk among the roots.

'I'll get him,' said Tobermory. 'Bungo, Orinoco, follow me.'

Their eyes had got used to the darkness and they plunged through the bushes to where the tree was balancing like a see-saw with all the branches at one end and Tomsk at the other. It was caught in the fork of another tree, and Tobermory shinned up it and then pulled the other two Wombles after him.

'I'll slide down towards Tomsk,' he said. 'You two hold the tree steady here.'

Orinoco and Bungo edged round, one on either side of the balancing tree, and braced their back paws against it and wound their front paws round the two branches, and then very slowly and cautiously Tobermory slid down the wet trunk, which shook and shivered and groaned and then began to tip down towards the ground. Tomsk, who had been jolted and jarred and shaken almost out of his senses, just clung on until he heard Tobermory's heavy breathing, and two strong paws very gently but firmly unclasped his own. And then with a cry and a thud Tomsk fell to the ground and lay there.

'Up you get,' said Great Uncle Bulgaria's voice,

and Tomsk looked up, and through the dripping twigs he saw a sou'wester and a pair of spectacles and a storm lantern. So he got up, but very stiffly, and his teeth were chattering with cold and tiredness.

'March,' said Great Uncle Bulgaria. 'One two, one two, back to the burrow with you.'

'The tree,' said Tomsk in a whisper.

'It fell away from the burrow, so there's nothing to worry about,' said Great Uncle Bulgaria briskly. 'Now *I* don't want to get wet through at my time of life, even if you do. Hurry up, there's a good Womble.'

And so a very weary, wet and bedraggled Tomsk shuffled through the bushes to the door of the burrow where he was joined by the others.

'It wasn't my fault, really it wasn't,' said Tomsk, who could hardly keep his eyes open, and who was yawning yawn after yawn so that his face felt as if it were splitting in two.

' 'Course it wasn't,' said Great Uncle Bulgaria. 'In with you. My word, what a sight you are, to be sure. I've never seen such a drowned-looking Womble in my life before.'

'I'll leave *two* dirty pawmarks this time,' said Tomsk, looking doubtfully at Tobermory.

'Well, the floor'll clean, I suppose,' barked Tobermory who, like Great Uncle Bulgaria, was showing his relief at finding Tomsk all in one piece by being very gruff.

'And there are cracks in the wall. I sort of made one of them,' went on Tomsk, who liked to take troubles one at a time.

'So I noticed,' agreed Tobermory. 'That tree'll make nice useful props. I've thought for a long

43

time that we needed some new building in this bit of the burrow. We'll start on it first thing in the morning. Bungo, Orinoco, pick up those boots and raincoats and put them in the Workshop. Then get a broom and sweep up this lot and shut the door. I'll nail a board across the bottom and that'll hold the mud back for the present.'

In any other circumstances Bungo and Orinoco might well have started grumbling at this point, but for once both those young Wombles felt thoroughly subdued, so they hurried off without a word to do as they were told, and by the time they had finished they were yawning almost as much as Tomsk had been.

'He must have been hanging on to that tree for hours,' said Orinoco, leaning on his broom.

'Hours and hours,' agreed Bungo.

The two young Wombles looked at each other, thinking their own thoughts. Would either of them have been brave enough or determined enough to do the same thing? They weren't at all sure about it, so they both decided to keep quiet on the subject.

'I tell you what,' said Bungo, 'let's go and clear up that mess we made in the Workshop. We might as well while we're at it.'

'I'm ever so hungry,' said Orinoco. 'Oh, all right then. Perhaps if we do Great Uncle Bulgaria won't be too furious with us.'

As it happened the wet paper fight in the Workshop was never mentioned again, although the threat of it did hang over the heads of Bungo and Orinoco for some while. Great Uncle Bulgaria watched them with a thoughtful expression and once or twice he had to put up his paw to hide a smile when he noticed the new, respectful way in which they now treated Tomsk.

'Ho-hum,' said Great Uncle Bulgaria to himself and got out the plans which Tobermory had made for strengthening the burrow against further tree falls, landslides and floods.

'Concrete,' muttered Great Uncle Bulgaria, reading Tobermory's neat list of building materials. 'Now where could we Wombles possibly find some concrete, I wonder . . . ?'

CHAPTER 5

BUNGO AND THE CONCRETE MIXER

There's a saying that troubles always come in threes, but when Tobermory happened to mention this rather unwisely to Great Uncle Bulgaria the old Womble said crossly, 'I'm perfectly well aware of it. And *I'd* like to point out that there's another motto *you* might do well to remember. Never meet trouble halfway.'

'There's going to *be* trouble, all the same,' said Tobermory, who always liked to look on the black side of things. He took his screwdriver from behind his ear and tapped the map on the wall. 'And *that*'s where it'll come. Good morning.'

And he went off leaving Great Uncle Bulgaria scowling and looking so fierce that when pretty little Alderney brought him in his mid-morning cup of hot bracken juice, she was quite scared and nearly upset it.

'Do you think something dreadful's going to

happen?' Alderney asked Bungo when he came out of the Workshop. 'Great Uncle Bulgaria looked ever so cross.'

'Never,' said Bungo. 'Don't you worry; we working Wombles'll look after everything.'

'I'm a working Womble too,' said Alderney, who had just started helping in the kitchens. She wasn't allowed to do much yet, but it made her feel very important when she was sent off with the trolley piled high with cakes, buns and biscuits and a big steaming urn of bracken juice. She did it twice a day, in the middle of the mornings and the afternoons, and as the Common was still very wet and muddy Great Uncle Bulgaria had ordered all work there to be stopped for the time being. So every working Womble was now employed in the burrow, either sorting in the Workshop or helping Tobermory put up wooden planks to strengthen the walls, ceilings and floors. This meant, of course, that Alderney was kept very busy, as there's nothing like sawing, hammering and sorting to put an edge on a Womble's appetite. Or anybody else's, for that matter.

'I wouldn't mind having your job,' said Orinoco, squeezing through the queue and looking at the food with his eyes glistening.

'There wouldn't be anything left for anybody else if you did,' said Bungo.

At which everybody else laughed and Orinoco turned his back and pretended not to hear as he carefully chose the three largest chocolate and peppermint buns. Alderney stopped looking anxious and went off down the passage ringing the bell at the side of her trolley so that the other Wombles would know she was coming.

47

However, in spite of his firm words, Bungo's mind was bothered by doubts. He was sensible and observant enough to notice that some of the floors had sunk a little and that every now and then a few drops of water would drip through the ceilings. It gave him a nasty feeling in his inside to realise that the nice comfortable burrow he had known all his life might not be so safe after all. It even made him lose his appetite a bit, so that he couldn't eat all his berry biscuit; but as Orinoco generously offered to finish it for him it wasn't wasted.

As soon as work was over, Bungo went to sit near some of the older Wombles in the Common Room. And by keeping his ears open and his mouth shut—which was a great effort for Bungo—he soon learnt that what was needed to make everything safe again was some stuff mysteriously called concrete.

'What is it?' Bungo asked Tomsk.

'White stuff,' said Tomsk somewhat breathlessly. He was doing his exercises, lying on his back and pedalling with his feet in the air.

'Like flour?' asked Bungo.

'Sort of, I think,' said Tomsk, rolling over and starting on his press-ups. 'One, two, three, four . . .'

'Flour's what you make cakes out of,' volunteered Orinoco. 'I don't think you use it for buildings and things. Do you know, it makes me feel quite tired watching Tomsk. I think I'll just have . . .'

'Forty winks,' said Bungo, and went to find Alderney, who was washing up.

'What's concrete?' Bungo asked, without much hope of a helpful reply.

'I don't know,' said Alderney, wiping her face

with the back of her paw. 'Would you like to dry for me?'

'Busy,' said Bungo, and braced himself to have a word with Tobermory.

Tobermory's face was even more gloomy than usual and he said gruffly, 'Don't you go worrying your head with things that don't concern you, young Womble. Now get out from under my paws, do.'

'How can I help if nobody'll tell me anything?' Bungo grumbled to himself, and then because he disliked being kept indoors for days on end he decided to go and have a look at the outside world. He took a pair of boots and an oilskin and a large hat and went off very stealthily, taking care to avoid the main door, as there was still some sawing and hammering going on there. Instead Bungo used one of the smaller, more deserted passages which went past the place where Tobermory's electric motors hummed and sang to each other and there were large notices on the doors saying:

DANGER. KEEP OUT!!!

Bungo had no intention of going in, and soon he was in a part of the burrow which was hardly ever used. It was a little frightening, for the lights were dim here, and there was no sound at all apart from a distant rumbling and crashing. This strange noise grew slowly louder and when Bungo opened the door which led to the Common it was very, very loud indeed. Even the ground was shaking with it, and Bungo looked as though he was doing a kind of bouncing dance as he parted the bushes and looked out.

At once he saw where all the din was coming from. He was very near the edge of the Common and there were only a few small trees between him and the road. Bungo's eyes widened as he watched the traffic hurtling past. It had actually stopped raining, but there was a kind of mistiness in the air as though it was full of millions of tiny drops of water. And as the cars went past making a soft *shushing* sound they sent up great sheets of dirty spray from the puddles.

'Oh my,' said Bungo, and wriggled further out into the open.

An enormous great red thing came down the road. It was glowing with lights and it was quite the largest object Bungo had ever seen close to. It appeared to be coming straight for him and Bungo gulped and dived head first back into the bushes. The thing roared and rattled past without taking any notice of him, and as Bungo slowly lifted his head he realised that it was no monster, but only an ordinary London bus.

'Ho-hum,' said Bungo, trying to sound like Great Uncle Bulgaria, and he dusted a few leaves off his coat and stepped out jauntily into the open. Opposite him, on the other side of the road, was a strange-looking machine, and as Bungo had never seen anything quite like it before he was puzzled and curious. Being Bungo he just had to have a closer look, but how was he to get across the road? His bright little eyes searched this way and that and then he noticed a yellow light flashing on and off beside a black and white path which was painted across the road. When a Human Being—it was an elderly man—stepped on this path all the cars stopped for him to cross over.

'Now or never,' said Bungo, and scampered out of the bushes and on to the path before he could lose his nerve. There was a dreadful screaming, tearing sound as cars coming from both directions drew up, or tried to. They skidded and skittered about, but somehow managed to avoid hitting each other, and several of the drivers leant out of their windows and shook their fists furiously at Bungo. Bungo waved back and went over to have a closer look at the machine. It was very dirty and splattered with mud, but on the sides he could just make out the words:

CONCRETE MIXER

Bungo was beside himself with excitement. He had found the one thing which the Wimbledon Wombles needed most in the world. Alone and unaided he had discovered the magical concrete. It's true that it did not look very exciting and it certainly smelt rather dull. What about its taste?

Bungo put out his paw and scraped a little of the fine, gritty stuff off the machine, sniffed it and then put it on his tongue. He spat it out at once. Horrible, you certainly couldn't make cakes out of THAT.

'Oh, I'm clever,' Bungo sang to himself. 'I'm so clever and fearless and brave. One, two, three . . .'

And over the crossing he danced, making a cyclist swerve into the pavement and almost into a letter box.

'I'll have the law on you!' the cyclist shouted.

'I'm so clever and fearless and brave . . .' sang a voice in the distance, and Bungo's sou'wester vanished into the bushes on the Common. He ran

51

all the way back, and a quarter of an hour later an extremely breathless Womble was standing in the Workshop with his lungs heaving and his tongue hanging out.

'C-c-concrete,' said Bungo, leaning up against Tobermory's table and panting.

'What about it?' snapped Tobermory, who had just hit his paw with a hammer, and was sucking it and blowing on it by turns.

'F-f-found some,' said Bungo.

Tobermory dropped the hammer, narrowly missing his toes, and leant across the table and gripped hold of Bungo's oilskins.

'If you're pulling my paw . . .' he said grimly.

'I'm not, honestly,' said Bungo, between pants. 'I found some. Lots of it. There's a machine that makes it and . . .'

'Come with me,' said Tobermory, and Bungo found himself once again being propelled towards Great Uncle Bulgaria's room, only this time he was not in disgrace, as he tried to show the other Wombles by nodding and smiling at them as he passed. He was still too breathless to speak properly.

'Calm down,' said Great Uncle Bulgaria. 'Now then, young Bungo, can you show me on this map where exactly—*exactly* mind—you found this machine?'

Bungo peered at the map which was spread across the table and found the black and white path.

'There,' he said, pointing.

Great Uncle Bulgaria and Tobermory breathed over his shoulders, and then all the excitement and triumph went out of Bungo with a rush as Great Uncle Bulgaria said crossly, 'But, you silly young Womble, that's not ON the Common. We can't tidy up concrete on the far side of the road.'

'Oh,' said Bungo, and felt himself shrinking.

'The need is desperate,' said Tobermory in a low voice.

'It would be stealing,' said Great Uncle Bulgaria in a still lower voice, and he shook his head, 'and Wombles never steal. Borrow sometimes, yes, but not take. Or in times of dire necessity there's barter or . . .'

'Or . . .' said Tobermory.

The two older Wombles looked at each other and Great Uncle Bulgaria slowly stroked the snow-white fur behind his ears while Bungo looked at them with his mouth turned right down at the corners.

'*Dire* necessity?' said Great Uncle Bulgaria.

'Astonishingly dire,' said Tobermory.

'The Workshop,' said Great Uncle Bulgaria,

'and make haste. Bungo, call together all the strongest Wombles and tell them to report to the Common Room in raincoats and carrying . . . ?' He glanced at Tobermory, who had taken a piece of paper and a pencil out of his apron pocket and was making notes.

'Buckets and spades,' said Tobermory.

'Buckets and spades,' said Bungo, who hadn't the slightest idea what was going on, but was starting to feel excited all over again.

Great Uncle Bulgaria went hobbling off down the passage with his shawl flying out behind him, and the moment he and Tobermory reached the Workshop he went straight to a large suitcase with MONEY—ENGLISH written on the side, while Tobermory made for his own small office and began to sort through a large number of magazines and books.

'*The Woodcarver's Friend*,' muttered Tobermory. 'No good. Ah, *Architect's Review*, better. *Builders' Merchant's Omnibus*, even better. *Pearsons, Porridge and Pullan's Price List*, best of all! Ah, ha!'

'Four pounds ninety-nine pence,' said Great Uncle Bulgaria quietly to himself. He had pulled a high carpenter's stool over to the table, and was perched up on it with the money before him, sorting it into neat little piles.

'And carry three, multiply by six,' said Tobermory, doing more sums as he checked the price list with one paw.

'Bless me, a Queen Victoria shilling,' said Great Uncle Bulgaria, forgetting the urgency of the moment as he gazed mistily at the old coin. 'I remember being taken to see her when she came out to the Common for a review of the troops. I had a flag to wave and a sailor's hat with HMS DREADNOUGHT on it. Happy days.'

'It'll come to forty-one pounds twelve pence,' said Tobermory. 'That'll be enough concrete to re-do the foundations, make good the cracks, and leave me two bags over for emergencies.'

'We mustn't cheat,' said Great Uncle Bulgaria. 'Better make it forty-one pounds fifteen pence just to be on the right side. It'll leave us with hardly anything, but we'll just have to manage. Still, there's usually plenty of money left lying about in the spring. Right, old friend, I leave the next part of the operation in your capable paws.'

'I suppose it had better be tonight?' Tobermory said.

'No time like the present,' said Great Uncle Bulgaria, getting down stiffly from the stool. 'Besides, they might move on tomorrow. There's a lot of building going on down by Tibbet's Corner, with the road widening scheme, and that would be a far more difficult place for us . . . ahem,' he coughed delicately behind his paw, 'for us from a *business* point of view.'

'Quite,' agreed Tobermory. 'Shall we go, then?'

Bungo had done his job well; for the Common Room was full of Wombles in oilskins, sou'westers and boots. The whispering died down as Great Uncle Bulgaria and Tobermory came in and everybody looked at them expectantly.

'Fellow Wombles,' said Great Uncle Bulgaria, who had forgotten that he had put Tobermory in charge of everything: he never could resist making a speech. 'It has come to our ears that some concrete is available on the other side of the Common. We intend to buy it.'

55

'Oh,' said Bungo, light dawning on him. Tobermory gave him a look, and Bungo sank out of sight behind Tomsk.

'Tobermory has worked out exactly how much it will cost and furthermore we are going to leave a present of fifty pence for any inconvenience we may cause. You will form yourselves into a line— everyone has a bucket and spade, I take it?'

A whole forest of buckets and spades were raised above the sou'westers.

'Good. I must impress upon you all that silence, efficiency and obedience are vital. Tobermory will be in command on the site.'

Tobermory nodded gravely and led the way down the passage. Not to another living Womble would he have admitted that in his raincoat pocket he had a small booklet called *Everything A Concrete Worker Should Know*. But as he walked rapidly down the winding corridors he kept taking little looks at it, and as he was a technician at heart he felt that by the time they emerged on to the Common he would know how to work a mixer. He hoped.

The evening rush of traffic was long since over and as it was a nasty cold damp night there were few people about. With their buckets hung over one arm, their shovels over their shoulders, the Wombles squelched across the grass and then over the crossing.

Flickering red lamps had been placed round the building site by a nightwatchman and Tobermory's eyes gleamed as he saw the stacks of timber and tools. Still, this was not the moment for idle dreams.

'Wombles, space yourselves out,' Tobermory

56

said in a low whisper. 'Tomsk, come with me, and remember to keep quiet whatever happens!'

Tomsk nodded violently, so violently that his sou'wester slid down over his eyes and he nearly walked straight into the mixer. Tobermory took a quick glance at his booklet, and then studied the fat bags of double brown paper which were stacked under a tarpaulin, each of them neatly labelled.

'One-to-three-to-six,' muttered Tobermory, reading one of the labels.

'What does it mean?' whispered Tomsk, almost treading on Tobermory's heels.

'One part of cement to three parts of sand and six parts of stone. It's a mixture which is right for foundations of mass concrete and similar work where great strength is not required,' replied Tobermory, who had learnt this bit by heart out of the booklet.

'Oh my,' breathed Tomsk, his admiration for Tobermory growing even greater than before.

'One-to-two-to-four is generally appropriate for reinforced concrete building construction and one-to-one-to-two is the richest of all and suitable for marine work and for reinforced conduits to convey water under pressure,' went on Tobermory, unable to resist the chance to air his brand new knowledge.

'Fancy,' said Tomsk, who hadn't the faintest idea what he was talking about, but who was enormously impressed all the same.

'Ho-hum,' said Tobermory. 'Well, well. We must get on with the job in hand, young Womble. One-Three-Six "Easy Mix" is the stuff we want. Give us a paw.'

They carried the bags over to the mixer one by

one, and then Tobermory filled a bucket with water from a tap at one side of the site and gave it to Tomsk, with orders to pour it into the mixer slowly once he was given the signal. Then he lined up all the other Wombles with their empty buckets, took a deep breath and cranked the engine.

Nothing happened.

A line of hopeful faces shadowed by sou'westers gazed trustingly at Tobermory, who felt a shiver of doubt run all the way up his back.

He cranked again, and this time the engine rumbled into life and Tomsk, who was standing right beside it, nearly jumped out of his fur. But he held his ground as the great barrel-like mixer slowly began to revolve and Tobermory poured in the contents of the bags and then ordered Tomsk to add the water. Just enough, not a drop too little or a trickle too much.

Rumble, rumble, rumble went the mixer, chewing its thick porridge and making a great deal of noise about it. More than one pair of Womble eyes slid sideways, wondering if the din would attract some human attention, and it says a great deal for their self-control that not one of them moved so much as a paw as the row went on and on, shattering the silence of the night.

However, the inhabitants of Wimbledon were so used to the roar and rumble of roadworks all around them, that they didn't even bother to draw their curtains and glance out. They just turned up their televisions and their radios and left the Wombles in peace.

'Time's up,' said Tobermory, whose eyes had been fastened to the enormous watch on his wrist. 'Tip it up, Tomsk. Slowly. You there, Bungo, put your bucket by the lip of the mixer.'

Tomsk did as he was told and a great sludgy flood of white stuff went *slurp, slurp, slurp* into Bungo's bucket.

'Shovel it in, shovel it in,' ordered Tobermory. 'Gently does it. Oh lovely, glorious concrete. Next please. Now then, Bungo, back to the burrow, but carefully, don't you dare spill a drop.'

Into the waiting buckets went the wet, slodgy concrete. It went into plastic buckets and tin pails and jam jars with handles on them. And when it came to Orinoco's turn it slopped into a pudding basin, which had been the only thing he could find. Bungo had a very fancy tin pail with A PRESENT FROM RAMSGATE on the side, and Tomsk had an enormous galvanized bucket with WBC [Wimbledon Borough Council.] on it. Tobermory himself had a red bucket with SAND on the side.

Great Uncle Bulgaria, with his paws clasped on his stick, watched his Wombles at work and felt proud of them. A small, elderly man who was hurrying home through the wet dark night almost walked full tilt into him.

'So sorry,' he said.

'Don't mention it, my dear sir,' said Great Uncle Bulgaria.

'Working late, aren't you?' said the man timidly. He lived by himself and was often rather lonely, so he liked to exchange a few words with somebody if he got the chance.

'Rush job,' said Great Uncle Bulgaria. 'All this rain's done a lot of damage.'

'Too true,' said the man. 'It never rained like this when I was young.'

'I quite agree with you,' said Great Uncle

59

Bulgaria. 'Well, I mustn't detain you, sir. Good evening.'

'Good evening to *you*, sir,' said the elderly man, and walked on, much impressed by the quick, efficient way in which the work was being done.

'That's it,' said Tobermory, switching off the mixer for the last time and shaking his paws, because his fur was full of sticky pieces of wet concrete. 'Home, everyone, fast as you can, before it sets fast.'

But he spoke to the empty air, for the last of the Wombles was even now vanishing across the black and white path, and there was only Great Uncle Bulgaria left, and he silently handed up a large brown paper parcel which Tobermory placed carefully beneath the tarpaulin. Inside it was the money, a list of the bags used, and a short polite note explaining what had happened. It was signed, *Your respectful and obedient servant, Bulgaria Coburg Womble* and to this day the foreman on that building site hasn't been able to make head or tail of what it was all about.

It was an extremely busy night for the Wombles, for under Tobermory's directions they dug up the badly cracked floors to make long, shallow pits which they lined with rubble and then filled with the concrete.

'Keep going, keep going,' urged Tobermory, one eye constantly on his watch, for he knew that the concrete would start to set within two hours, although it wouldn't become completely hard for forty-eight hours. The younger Wombles, including Orinoco and Bungo, were busy on the walls, filling in the cracks and smoothing them over, while Tomsk, as the tallest Womble, was given the job of dealing with cracked ceilings. To keep their strength up the kitchens were kept open all night and Alderney, with her bell ringing furiously on the trolley, was kept trotting backwards and forwards with hot drinks and snacks.

The whole burrow, in fact, was a humming, buzzing, busy hive of activity as bucketload after bucketload of concrete was used to make it strong and waterproof again. Tobermory somehow managed to be everywhere at once, directing, explaining and encouraging. And not one Womble, not even Orinoco, stopped working for a single minute, because every second was important.

The thin pale light of dawn was creeping silently across the Common by the time the last bucket had been emptied and the last shovel wiped clean and put away. As the Wombles, yawning and weary, made their way to bed, Great Uncle Bulgaria stood in his doorway, his paws clasped on his stick. He was very proud of them and for each one he had a kind word until at last only Tobermory was left.

'Well, old friend,' said Great Uncle Bulgaria, 'well done. Congratulations on a job magnificently planned and carried out. And now perhaps you'll believe me when I say it doesn't do to meet trouble halfway.'

'Be that as it may,' said Tobermory, who was so tired he was almost asleep on his paws, 'but don't you forget what *I* said. Troubles come in threes. Look.' And he pointed to a newly laid strip of concrete. Right across it was a line of pawmarks.

'That Bungo,' said Tobermory. 'I told him it was still soft, but he wouldn't listen.'

'And the third trouble?' asked Great Uncle Bulgaria.

Tobermory's usually dour face split into a smile.

'Orinoco,' he said. 'It was the pudding basin he was using that did it. He forgot that it was concrete he was carrying and he tasted some out of sheer force of habit. He thought it was some sort of cake.'

'Ho-hum,' said Great Uncle Bulgaria, 'perhaps that'll teach him to be less greedy in future, though I doubt it. Even *his* stomach won't take kindly to concrete. Well, goodnight, old friend.'

And very slowly, and with aching limbs but contented hearts, the two old Wombles made for their beds.

CHAPTER 6

ORINOCO AND THE RABBIT HOLE

Orinoco did have a nasty stomach ache for a couple of days but he soon forgot all about it and went back to eating as much as ever. Perhaps even more, to make up for lost time.

'You're getting dreadfully fat,' said Bungo.

'I'm not. I'm a fine figure of a Womble,' replied Orinoco. '*I* wouldn't like to be skinny.'

And he glanced meaningly at Bungo who, like all the other Wombles, was a nice, comfortable, round shape. This was because they were lucky enough to have an excellent cook called Madame Cholet. She wasn't really French, but when years ago the time had come for her to choose her name, she had picked out a town in France because she had once heard that was the country where the cooking was wonderful. She was small and round and cheerful, and she loved her work so much that she was always in the kitchen doing something.

Orinoco had once offered to go and help her, but Madame Cholet had dug him in the ribs with a wooden spoon and said, 'Oh no. Your paws would be into everything.'

'No, honestly not,' said Orinoco, making his eyes look as large and truthful as he could. 'I really would help.'

'Hum,' said Madame Cholet, 'in that case we will give it a try. You shall help me for one week. It is agreed, yes?'

'Rather,' said Orinoco. 'Where do I start?' And he looked hopefully at a delicious stew which Madame Cholet was stirring. 'Shall I do that for you?'

'No. You must begin by learning something more simple. You shall top and tail the hawthorn berries. Then you can chop up some grass. After that there are the nettles which must be stripped off their stalks. Then you can peel the mushrooms and finally you must help Alderney with the washing-up. Here is an apron—my word, what a splendid waist you have—now please to begin.'

Poor Orinoco! He stuck it as long as he could, but no matter how hard he peeled and cut, stripped and chopped, there was always another job for him to do and none of the food with which he was working tasted at all nice till it was cooked.

The funny thing was that by the end of that week in the kitchen with Madame Cholet he was actually thinner than when he started. And what was more there was never a chance to slip off to the pantry or the larder to have a nice forty winks, because Madame Cholet seemed to have her eyes in the back of her head and she would whisk him off to the next job.

So Orinoco admitted that he was beaten and Madame Cholet cuffed him affectionately round the ears and gave him half a bar of chocolate and sent him back to Tobermory. It was really quite a relief to get out on to the Common again, and it took Orinoco another week to recover his strength. He was still recovering with his battered old hat tied over his head with the long woollen scarf when Bungo came bouncing up to him and said, 'Look what I've found.'

'It's an egg,' said Orinoco, opening one eye. It was really quite a nice day for December, with plenty of bright, if not very warm, sunshine.

'At this time of year?' said Bungo. 'No, it's a ball, but it won't bounce much. Look . . .' and he threw it hard on the grass, which it hit with a thud, bounced just a little and then rolled away.

'It's a goluff ball,' said Orinoco.

'What's that?'

'There's a game called goluff. Human Beings play it. They hit those little balls with sticks and shout at each other. Tobermory's got hundreds of those things, and the sticks too.'

'Why do they shout at each other?' asked Bungo. His basket was full and he felt he could take it easy for five minutes. Not like Orinoco, who worked the other way round and took it easy for fifty-five minutes and then worked like mad in the remaining five.

'Human Beings like shouting,' said Orinoco through his hat. 'Haven't you noticed *that* yet? They shout when they play goluff and they shout at their dogs and they shout at their children. They like it.'

'Very odd,' said Bungo, wrinkling his forehead,

for Wombles, although they are great talkers, are quiet creatures by nature. 'I wonder if we could play goluff?'

But Orinoco's only answer was a gentle snore, so Bungo put the question away to the back of his mind and waited until he caught Tobermory in a good mood.

'Goluff?' said Tobermory, who was working on a bicycle that a Human Being had dumped behind a bush. 'Oh, you mean *golf*. They play it for exercise, even quite old people. You take one of these little balls—hold on and I'll show you.'

And Tobermory disappeared into one of his small storerooms and then reappeared with a wicker hamper that was full to the brim with small golf balls. Under his arm was a stick with a metal piece sticking out at the end.

'Like this,' said Tobermory, putting a ball down on the floor and swinging the stick over the top of it. 'This is called addressing the ball.'

'What do you address it as?' asked Bungo, deeply interested. It really was astonishing how little one knew about Human Beings even if one had been a Womble of the world for three months.

'Ball, I suppose,' said Tobermory. 'Now then, ball, I'm going to hit you,' and he gave it a gentle tap and the ball rolled across the floor and into a milk carton which was lying on its side.

'Let me, let me,' pleaded Bungo, wriggling down from the work table.

'Not in here you don't,' said Tobermory. 'Try outside in the passage. And before you hit it, shout "four".'

'Why?'

'Why, why, why; you and your questions, young

66

Womble. Because you do, that's why. Off with you, I'm busy.'

And Tobermory returned to his bicycle and began to unscrew it and take it to pieces. He was always short of bolts, nuts and bits of wire. So Bungo took the stick out into the corridor and put the ball down on the ground and shouted 'four', which seemed a bit silly, and then he swung the stick with all his might. The next thing he knew he was sitting on the ground and the ball was still in the same place.

'Missed,' muttered Bungo, scrambling to his feet.

'Hallo, what are you doing?' asked Tomsk, coming round the corner. He had finished his exercises and he wasn't on duty until the evening, so like Bungo he had some time to spare.

'Playing golf.'

'Can I play too?'

'Yes, if you like,' said Bungo in an offhand way. 'Go and get a stick from Tobermory. And your own ball.'

Tomsk did better than that, for Tobermory had gone to his office and found a tattered little book called *How To Play Good Golf In Six Easy Lessons!* and he handed this over as well.

'It's early yet,' said Bungo, who had just succeeded in hitting the ball and had narrowly missed breaking an electric light bulb into the bargain, 'so there won't be any Humans about. Let's go and play outside.'

They found the place where the Humans usually played and settled down to have a go themselves. Although the pictures in the book made it seem quite easy to do, Bungo and Tomsk soon found that it was extremely difficult.

'The ball's too small,' grumbled Bungo, when he missed it for the third time. He was getting rather tired of sitting down with a thump on the frosty ground.

'Oh, I don't think so,' said Tomsk in his slow way, and he planted his paws apart, just like the picture in the book and swung back his stick and hit the ball with all his might. As he was very strong the ball lifted up into the air and fairly sailed along until it finally came down in some bushes beside the course. There was a howl and a moment later a very indignant face appeared underneath an old straw hat.

'That hit me!' said Orinoco.

'Sorry,' said Tomsk.

'What are you doing there?' asked Bungo.

'Nothing much,' said Orinoco, twisting round in a rather uneasy fashion.

'I'm coming to see,' said Bungo, and went lolloping across to Orinoco, who dived back into the bushes, which quivered slightly. Tomsk thudded over to look for his ball and arrived just after Bungo, who was ferreting around with his stick.

'Now look here,' said Orinoco, 'if a Womble can't just have a nice nap for a moment or two, I don't know what the world's coming to.'

Orinoco was sitting down with his paws folded in his lap and his paper carrier bag at his side. There were one or two coloured wrappers in it, a comb and a shoe for the left foot.

'Just sunning myself, you know,' said Orinoco airily. 'That's all.'

'Come and have some exercise,' said Bungo,

pulling him to his back paws. 'You're getting too fat.'

Orinoco looked rather anxious, but after a moment's hesitation he gave in and followed the other two on to the course. He was even more hopeless at the game than Bungo and he panted and snorted as he was made to walk from one hole to another, blowing out his cheeks and grumbling when he had the breath left to do so.

'You'll never be able to eat any Christmas dinner,' said Bungo.

'Yes, I will.'

'No, you won't.'

'Are you going to have a fight?' Tomsk asked with interest. He had been hitting golf balls in all directions and thoroughly enjoying himself. He came ambling back now, looking at the two angry young Wombles with polite interest.

'No,' said Orinoco furiously, 'it's just this silly game. I don't care if I can't play it, so there,' and he picked up Bungo's stick and swung it with all his might and by some lucky chance the metal part connected with the ball and it went flying up into the air in a lovely great arc.

'Oh, well played,' said Tomsk, dropping his own stick and clapping his paws together.

'Not bad,' Bungo agreed grudgingly.

'There, told you so,' said Orinoco. 'I can hit it all right, but not in the right direction and—OH!'

And he dropped his stick and began to run very fast (for him) towards the bushes where the ball had landed.

'Mad,' said Tomsk.

'Batty,' agreed Bungo.

A howl of such awful misery reached their ears

69

that both Wombles felt their fur rise on end. They raced for the bushes, but there was no sign of Orinoco, only the howling, which was now very muffled.

'There,' said Tomsk, who had seen one of the bushes moving, and he plunged in with Bungo close behind him. Tomsk parted the bracken and then stepped back right into Bungo as he saw before him the back paws of Orinoco waving in the air.

'What is it?' whispered Bungo.

'Smee,' said Orinoco's muffled voice. 'I'm stuck.'

'But what are you doing down there?' asked Bungo.

'Get me out,' wailed Orinoco, kicking harder than ever.

'You take one leg and I'll take the other,' ordered Bungo. He and Tomsk seized a paw each and pulled with all their might, but Orinoco had spoken the absolute truth: he was completely wedged in a rabbit hole.

'Get a spade,' ordered Bungo, and off went Tomsk, running across the golf course with his arms tucked into his sides and his head well back, just like a four-minute miler. He vanished over the skyline and Bungo was left with the kicking paws of Orinoco.

'Never mind, old chap,' said Bungo, trying not to laugh. 'We'll soon get you out. But what were you doing down there anyway?'

'Nothing much,' said Orinoco's muffled voice. 'Just looking, you know.'

'What for?'

'The ball.'

70

'But the ball's here,' said Bungo, whose sharp eyes had just spotted it lying under some dead leaves.

'Oh, oh, oh,' howled Orinoco, kicking more than ever. 'It's a judgement on me, that's what it is. You were quite right, Bungo. I'm a fat, greedy Womble and I've got my just deserts.' And he suddenly went alarmingly limp.

'Orinoco?' said Bungo. There was no reply. 'Orinoco?' said Bungo more loudly. 'Orinoco—speak to me.' But Orinoco didn't move. Bungo went stiff with fright and then he noticed that one leg was twitching slightly so he picked up a twig and just ran it down the sole of Orinoco's paw. The paw jumped and Orinoco's voice said furiously, 'Don't tickle, it's not fair.'

'Well, at least you're still alive,' said Bungo.

'Only just though,' Orinoco said feebly.

Fortunately, Tomsk, not in the least out of breath, reappeared at this moment with a spade. He began to dig all round the hole and in a very few moments he had loosened the frosty earth enough to make it crumble.

'We'll pull together,' Bungo said. 'A leg each and one, TWO, THREE!'

And the next second Orinoco came out of the hole with exactly the same noise as a cork makes when it's taken out of a flask. His head, shoulders and front paws were covered in mud and leaves, and clutched in his arms was a lemonade bottle.

'You've got a secret larder down there,' Bungo said severely, and Orinoco brushed some of the mud off his face and looked down at his toes.

'Just one or two quite little things,' he said in a small voice. 'A Womble of my build needs a few

71

little extras to keep up his strength.'

'I'm going to have a look,' said Bungo, and although he was not slim himself he was nevertheless a great deal less chubby than Orinoco, so he had no trouble in wriggling into the hole and reappearing a few moments later with two chocolate bars, a bag of buns and a packet of chewing gum. Orinoco looked from the food to the other two Wombles and heaved an enormous sigh. Then without a word he got to his paws, dusted the leaves off his coat and set out for the burrow with Tomsk and Bungo following him.

'I don't think we'd better tell on him, do you?' asked Bungo, who had been turning matters over in his mind. He was sure that Orinoco had learnt his lesson, for it must have been extremely nasty to be stuck down a rabbit hole.

'Tell what?' asked Tomsk, who had been thinking about golf and the slice he was getting in his swing.

'Nothing really,' said Bungo and followed Orinoco into the burrow. Orinoco looked anxiously at his friend and when Bungo shook his head slightly Orinoco blew out his cheeks with relief and went to hand in his food to Tobermory. He stayed in the Workshop for a very long time and when he came out he had a rather smug expression on his round face.

'Tomorrow morning,' he said, laying his paw against one side of his nose. 'Meet me tomorrow morning by Queen's Mere.'

Bungo hadn't the faintest idea what he was up to, but Orinoco refused to say another word and went back into the Workshop and shut the door. Bungo stayed outside and heard a lot of banging and hammering and a great deal of whispering which made him more curious than ever, but Tobermory had hung a DO NOT DISTURB sign on the door, so he had to swallow his curiosity and go off and have a game of Wombles and Ladders with Alderney instead.

This is really a teaching game for very young Wombles and it was designed by Great Uncle Bulgaria and built by Tobermory. It's played in a large room where a great many ladders of all shapes and sizes are joined together with bars, planks and branches. You have to start at one end of the room, climb up the first ladder to the top, scramble along a pole and down the next ladder and then up the one next to it and so on. While all this is going on, an older Womble squeezes away at an accordion and the moment he stops you have to stop too. If you're halfway up a ladder then you have to go right back to the beginning and start again. The first Womble to reach the bottom of the last ladder is the winner.

This is how very young Wombles are taught to climb and although Bungo considered himself rather old for the game he soon joined in and enjoyed himself very much.

Early the next morning he picked up his basket and went off to Queen's Mere. It was going to be another lovely, clear but cold day and the ducks were out swimming up and down and the sparrows were pecking at the hard ground looking hopefully for worms. And it was then that Bungo saw a very curious sight.

It was Orinoco taking some exercise. But he wasn't playing golf or running or doing press-ups. He was riding a bicycle. A bicycle with a very low saddle because he had such short fat legs, so he and Tobermory had fitted a special saddle to make pedalling easier.

'Look at me,' called out Orinoco. 'This is the way to take some exercise. Splendid for the muscles. Wonderful for the constitution. Much better than silly old golf.'

And he sailed past Bungo ringing his bell and pedalling with all his might. So if any Human Being should be up on the Common early enough one morning they too might see a very strange sight. A round, not-quite-so-fat-as-before creature seated on a most extraordinary bicycle and riding across the grass for all he's worth. Orinoco doesn't do it every day of course, but he does cycle fairly often.

Getting stuck in a rabbit hole can be a very upsetting experience.

CHAPTER 7

THE CHRISTMAS PARTY AND
MR D. SMITH

The Christmas party was an enormous success. Madame Cholet cooked a better dinner than ever before, Great Uncle Bulgaria made a very funny speech, and Tobermory did conjuring tricks that were really quite astounding. How he made a golf ball come out of Tomsk's ear, how he made Alderney vanish, and how he sawed Bungo in half no Womble could understand. And as if that wasn't enough excitement there was the present-giving to follow.

For the last few days before Christmas every Womble, however young, had been allowed out on to the Common to find a gift. This is an old, long-established custom and although December is not a good time of year in which to discover things, somehow there never seems to be a shortage. Of course, some Wombles say among themselves that before the great gift hunt starts Tobermory and Great Uncle Bulgaria have been seen to slip out with loaded baskets in their paws on the evening beforehand. But naturally this rumour is kept from the youngest Wombles and the fact remains that they always do find something.

Whatever that something is, it's always kept a secret and shown only to Tobermory or Madame Cholet—who besides being such a wonderful cook is also very good at sewing and mending—and that something is always turned into a very nice present. All the presents are then packed up in brightly coloured paper and placed in an enormous tub and after the meal and the speech and the conjuring tricks every Womble gathers round and, starting with the youngest, plunges his or her paw into it and pulls out a gift.

And even more astonishing were the gifts which the elderly gentleman found. But then he was feeling very astonished altogether and his story really starts about three days before Christmas on a very bright, crisp afternoon.

The name of the elderly gentleman was Mr D. Smith and he was the same person who had talked to Great Uncle Bulgaria on the night of the Concrete Mixer Expedition. He happened to read in the local paper about the strange way in which the concrete had vanished from the building site and exactly the correct money (plus the fifty pence tip) had been discovered by the site foreman. He was very puzzled by this and as he had plenty of time to spare, being retired from his job, he went along to see the foreman. The foreman listened to what the elderly gentleman had to say and then pushed back his cap and said, 'Workmen, did you say?'

'Very small workmen wearing oilskins, boots and sou'westers,' said the elderly gentleman. 'One of them spoke to me most politely. He had white whiskers.'

'*I* see,' said the foreman in exactly that tone of voice which meant he didn't see at all. 'Well, thank you very much, sir . . .'

And he went off winking at all the other workmen, and the elderly gentleman looked rather sad and went for a walk on the Common. He was becoming used to people treating him as though he had to be humoured and that only made him feel sadder than ever. So, although there was a decided nip in the air, he went and sat on the bench where he always went, and looked at the bare bushes and trees and sighed more than ever.

And it was there that, three days before Christmas, Great Uncle Bulgaria met him. It was a lovely, sharp afternoon and Great Uncle Bulgaria had decided to slip out for a short walk before supper. He also wanted to see that all the young working Wombles were doing their jobs properly and, if possible, to catch a glimpse of Orinoco on his bicycle, which, Tobermory had assured him, was a sight not to be missed.

Both Great Uncle Bulgaria and the elderly gentleman arrived at the bench at the same moment. On this occasion the old Womble was wearing a balaclava helmet, an overcoat which reached to his toes, and fur-lined boots, for there was frost in the air and he tended to feel the cold these days.

'I beg your pardon,' said the elderly gentleman.

'No, after you, sir,' said Great Uncle Bulgaria.

'Good gracious me, surely we've met before?'

'Yes indeed,' said the elderly gentleman, recognising Great Uncle Bulgaria's white whiskers and round spectacles. 'It was—er ...'

'Exactly,' said Great Uncle Bulgaria. 'Lovely afternoon, isn't it? Just the right sort of weather for Christmas.'

'Christmas,' said the elderly gentleman with a sigh. 'I remember when I was young it always snowed about now.'

'So it did, so it did,' agreed Great Uncle Bulgaria, rubbing his gloves together. 'Tell me, sir, do you recall the great frost of ... let me see, was it '96 or '97?'

' '98,' said the elderly gentleman firmly. 'Ah, what a winter that was to be sure. Toboggan rides, the Thames was frozen over, and they put straw in the streets to stop the horses from sliding. Why, it seems only yesterday that ...'

As Great Uncle Bulgaria was the very soul of politeness he listened quietly to the elderly gentleman, nodding and saying 'Ah, quite', or 'Yes indeed', or 'How very true', whenever the occasion arose. The elderly gentleman was absolutely delighted to have such a splendid audience and after a while Great Uncle Bulgaria had to wriggle his feet inside his fur-lined boots to try and keep them warm, because the damp cold was seeping up through the frozen ground.

'Christmas WAS Christmas in those days,' said the elderly gentleman at last. 'Tell me, sir, have you any family?'

Great Uncle Bulgaria, whose mind had been wandering to other things, such as clue number three down in *The Times* crossword which had

78

been bothering him all day, replied a little absently.

'Family? Me? Oh yes, about two hundred and thirty of them.'

'I *beg* your pardon?' said the elderly gentleman.

'Altogether, that is,' said Great Uncle Bulgaria hastily, 'taking into account Great-Nephews and Nieces and Second Cousins Three Times Removed and so on. Do you not have a family yourself, sir?'

'No, sir,' said the elderly gentleman. 'I had one son, but he went to America many, many years ago to seek his fortune. The last letter I had from him was posted in a town called Butte in the state of Montana. That must have been twenty years ago . . .'

'Dear me,' said Great Uncle Bulgaria. 'So at Christmas you'll be—er—?'

'Oh, I shall be splendid, splendid,' said the elderly gentleman, suddenly jumping to his feet. 'Very pleased to have made your acquaintance again Mr—er?'

'Womble,' said Great Uncle Bulgaria.

Usually he didn't have much to do with Human Beings. They were too untidy, too noisy, and given to telling lies, but like all Wombles he had a very warm heart and he knew perfectly well that the elderly gentleman had just told a polite fib about being all right. Great Uncle Bulgaria thought fast and came to a decision.

'Ho-hum,' he said, stroking his white whiskers, '*should* you be free on Christmas evening and *should* you happen to be here I should be most honoured *should* you care to join me and my family for a small party.'

79

'Ah, well now,' said the elderly gentleman turning up his coat collar, for it had begun to sleet, 'that's very kind of you, sir, but I am rather fully engaged. However, *should* any of my arrangements fall through—perhaps I might avail myself of your generous invitation?'

'Quite, quite,' said Great Uncle Bulgaria. They said goodbye and the elderly gentleman went off across the Common, and the old Womble looked after him for a time and then shook his head and picked up his stick and went back to the burrow, and was so quiet and so sad for the rest of the evening that Tobermory became quite anxious, and sent Alderney off to the kitchen to make an extra sweet hot blackberry fruit juice. Great Uncle Bulgaria drank it down almost in one gulp and then said gravely, 'I'm glad *I*'m not a Human Being,' and stumped off to finish *The Times* [Great Uncle Bulgaria was re-reading *The Times* of July 1935 at this time. It was one of his favourite periods.] crossword.

Of course the elderly gentleman *was* there, exactly as Great Uncle Bulgaria had known he would be. He was carrying a small box done up in brightly coloured paper and he was wearing a high stiff collar with a great deal of starch in it, and a bowler hat which was green round the brim, and a very long overcoat.

'I managed to get away,' he said, not looking Great Uncle Bulgaria in the eye. 'My friends pleaded with me to stay, but I told them I didn't want to let you down, Mr Womble.'

'How very thoughtful,' said Great Uncle Bulgaria. 'This way, my dear sir,' and he took hold of the elderly gentleman's sleeve and gently pulled

80

him through the bushes and down to the main
door where Tomsk was waiting for them wearing a
paper hat and a very wide grin. The elderly
gentleman shook his paw and blinked and then
when he saw the other Wombles he very sensibly
came to the conclusion that of course it was all a
dream, but as it was a very pleasant one he might
as well enjoy it. Also the burrow—thanks to
Tobermory's new system of hot pipes—was
deliciously warm, and the elderly gentleman
couldn't recall the last time when he hadn't felt
chilled to the bone. So after a few doubtful
seconds he handed over his hat and coat to Tomsk
and put back his head and made up his mind to
have a wonderful time in this delightful dream.

The Wombles, who had all been warned
beforehand about Great Uncle Bulgaria's guest,
behaved splendidly and shook the visitor by the
hand, being careful to sheathe their claws before
they did so, and Alderney fetched him a very

beautiful-smelling hot drink, and Orinoco handed him a chocolate bun, and Bungo led him to a seat in the very centre of the long table.

The elderly gentleman ate and ate in a way which earned him Orinoco's deepest respect, and he roared with laughter at Great Uncle Bulgaria's speech and clapped like anything at Tobermory's conjuring tricks. And then came the great moment for the presents to be discovered, and he was made to go first and by some very strange coincidence what should he bring out of the tub but a most beautiful black umbrella!

'But that's . . .' said Orinoco, looking at Bungo.

'Yes, it is,' agreed Bungo, grinning from ear to ear.

And it was—the very same umbrella that had carried Orinoco high across the Common and had so nearly drowned him in the Queen's Mere. Only since those days Tobermory and Madame Cholet had both worked on it and now the spokes were all the right way round and the handle was polished until it shone like the sunrise and the black silk was clean and mended and looked as good as new.

'*Just* what I wanted,' said the elderly gentleman. 'Oh, *exactly* what I really needed.'

'Amazing,' said Great Uncle Bulgaria, sounding quite astounded.

'Astonishing,' murmured Tobermory.

'Do have another go,' prompted Alderney, 'please', and she tugged at the elderly gentleman's sleeve and whispered in his ear, and he smiled and put his hand down into the tub, and this time he came out with a large tin and inside it was a special blackcurrant cake, which is a very special cake indeed as you can eat it slowly slice by slice, and

82

even if it takes you six months it never goes stale, as the elderly gentleman subsequently discovered.

'One more for luck,' said Bungo and this time the elderly gentleman's hand came up with six white handkerchiefs, all clean and beautifully ironed and one of them actually had 'D. Smith' on the hem, which, as it was his name was really a remarkable coincidence, as everybody agreed.

'D for Donald, the same as my son,' said the elderly gentleman, and then added something more but in such a low voice that none of the Wombles could quite make out what it was, and Great Uncle Bulgaria took him gently by the arm and drew him over to a chair at the side of the Common Room, and they sat and watched the younger Wombles playing games and at the end of a particularly noisy round of Blind Womble's Buff the elderly gentleman, or Mr D. Smith, said, 'Best Christmas I've had in many a long year.'

'Is that so? Glad to hear it,' said Great Uncle Bulgaria, and then he clapped his paws together and everyone stopped laughing and dancing and Great Uncle Bulgaria said quietly, 'Listen.'

And everybody held their breath and listened and sure enough they could just hear the sound of distant singing.

'What is it?' asked Mr Smith, blowing his nose on one of the new handkerchiefs.

'Shall we go and see?' asked Great Uncle Bulgaria. They put on their coats and mufflers and, in Great Uncle Bulgaria's case, boots and gloves and a tartan shawl as well, and then they made their way down the long corridors, all of them decorated with paper chains and streamers and coloured lights, till they came to the main door, where Tomsk was on duty.

The moment Tomsk saw them all coming he opened the door and the sound of the voices grew louder, and as the Wombles came out on to the Common they saw that the ground was glittering white from a deep frost and that the stars were shining with a clear white light in the cold night sky. Beyond the edges of the Common the yellow lamps of London had turned the air to a misty amber, but where the Wombles stood there were no lights at all except for three small red lanterns which were held by a group of the youngest Wombles. Their small eyes and furry faces were lit by them and their paws shuffled a little nervously, but when they saw Great Uncle Bulgaria slowly coming out into the open followed by the tall figure of Tobermory and the round shape of Madame Cholet, they stopped fidgeting and cleared their throats and for a few moments there was silence apart from the distant roar of traffic which never stops, not even on Christmas Day. Then all the youngest Wombles fixed their eyes on their leader and took a very deep breath and began to sing in their small, clear voices one of the very old Christmas carols. They didn't always sing in tune and at least one of them forgot the words and had to go 'la la la' for a few lines, but nobody noticed and at the finish several of the older Wombles and Mr D. Smith had to blow their noses and stamp their feet and say things like 'It's cold tonight' and 'How clear the stars are, to be sure'.

'I must be getting back,' said Mr D. Smith. 'I can't tell you how much I've enjoyed this evening. How very, *very* much.'

'Delighted to have you,' said Great Uncle

Bulgaria, who had himself enjoyed having a long talk about The Good Old Days.

He nodded to Bungo and Tomsk, who took two of the red lanterns—which had WBC on them—and they led the elderly gentleman across the Common to the black and white path, and as he seemed to be in rather a dreamy state they crossed it with him and took him all the way back to the room where he lived.

'I can't begin to tell you . . .' he said.

'Please don't mention it,' said Bungo, half of whose mind was wondering if there would be any mince pies left by the time he and Tomsk returned to the burrow.

'Wonderful, wonderful evening,' said the elderly gentleman, and he went up to his cold room and went to bed and slept right through to the following morning, when he woke up and told the ceiling about the remarkable dream he had had. And the most astonishing part of it was that there on the table beside his bed was a blackcurrant cake, six handkerchiefs (one slightly used) and a splendid black silk umbrella. He never could quite account for all that and after a time he gave up trying and decided just to accept the fact that they were his and very nice too.

'But supposing he had told other Human Beings about us?' said Bungo, when he was helping Tobermory to put away the decorations for next year.

'They wouldn't have believed him,' said Tobermory. 'That's what comes of telling fibs, you see. You can't tell the difference between truth and stories in the end. Hand us those electric lights, young Womble, and stop asking questions for once in your life.'

'All right,' said Bungo cheerfully. 'Still, I'm glad that umbrella came in useful after all,' and he glanced at Orinoco, who was sweeping crumbs off the table.

'*Woof, bark, grrrrrr* to you,' said Orinoco, 'likewise Dalmatian dogs.'

And he tipped the last of the crumbs into his mouth and licked his lips with a satisfied smile.

CHAPTER 8

THE SNOW WOMBLE

Of course it was too much to expect that the young Wombles could go on behaving so well once the excitement of Christmas had worn off, while the Midsummer outing was still six months away, so when Bungo went off to work one morning and found that it was actually snowing something like pandemonium broke out.

'*I* can't control them,' said Tobermory.

'Shouldn't try if I were you,' said Great Uncle Bulgaria. Although he hadn't actually seen the snow himself, he could sense it in the atmosphere and it always made him feel uncommonly sleepy.

Tobermory muttered to himself and went back to the Workshop and began to tinker with a secret project that he had started on just before the Awful Rainstorms. He found it very soothing, and after a while he forgot all about the mutinous behaviour of the younger Wombles and settled down quite happily to oiling and greasing and taking apart and investigating whatever-it-was that he was so interested in.

Meanwhile Bungo and Orinoco and Alderney were having a look at this strange new outside world. None of them, not even Orinoco, had seen snow before and they found it the most wonderful stuff imaginable. For a start it looked so lovely as it lay glinting in the sunshine, and secondly it meant that all work was suspended out on the Common as no Human Beings, however forgetful, were going to drop or abandon their belongings on this clean white carpet.

'Look, look, look,' shouted Bungo, running down a slope and turning to glance over his shoulder at his own prints.

'Look, look, look,' called Alderney, and she put down her head and went head over heels, leaving a funny bumpy track behind her.

'Look, look, look,' cried Orinoco, and he lay down and rolled over faster and faster until he reached the bottom.

'You look like a snow Womble,' said Alderney, pulling him to his back paws.

'Let's build one,' said Orinoco.

'Not allowed,' said Bungo, who was gazing entranced at his own rather flat-footed pawmarks. There is something about leaving a trail of one's own pawmarks in the snow which is extremely exciting.

'Why not?' asked Alderney, sticking out her underlip and looking very sulky.

' 'Cause of them,' said Bungo, jerking his head towards the road at the side of the Common where the traffic was moving very slowly and the snow had already turned to a dirty yellow mush.

'You're a 'fraidy Womble; who's a 'fraidy Womble?' said Alderney, dancing round and round.

'I'm not!'

'It's like sugar icing,' said Orinoco dreaming, picking up handfuls of glittering, gleaming snow. He hadn't been able to get out recently on his bicycle because of the weather and he was growing stout once more.

'I'm *not* afraid,' said Bungo angrily, 'but if a Human Being found a snow Womble it could lead to all kinds of difficulties, so there.'

'Well, I'm not scared even if you are,' said Alderney, more unfairly still. And she began to pick up great pawfuls of snow and to pat them and mould them, with her little pink tongue hanging out of the corner of her mouth and her breath making steamy clouds in the cold, frosty air.

Bungo dug his heel in the ground and kicked some snow about and muttered under his breath. He knew he was in the right, but Alderney had a trick of making him feel stuffy and cowardly, and so after a moment or two he forgot Tobermory's lecture on the subject and went to help.

'It'll be the best snow Womble in the whole world,' said Alderney, giggling with excitement. 'I know, Bungo, let's make it . . .' and she whispered into his ear behind her paw.

'We couldn't,' said Bungo with his eyes popping.

'I'm not scared,' said Alderney, and began to shovel up snow faster than ever, and soon the two young Wombles were hard at work on Alderney's idea.

Now Tobermory's words had been very sensible,

for although someone like the elderly gentleman could be invited to the Womble's Christmas party and no harm done, he was the exception, for there are a great many Human Beings in the world who would not only say that Wombles don't exist, but who would go to an enormous amount of trouble to prove it. And it was these very people that Tobermory had in mind when he gave his lecture, as he knew that a great Womble Hunt (to show that there were no such creatures) might lead to discovery and disaster. Unfortunately, however, at this moment Tobermory was busy on something else and he did not notice when Bungo and Alderney returned to the burrow looking rather guilty and yet pleased with themselves at the same time. Orinoco, of course, hadn't noticed anything at all as he had been too busy trying to work out whether snow could be turned into icing sugar. As it looked so similar he was certain in his own mind that it could, and he hurried off to have a word with Madame Cholet on the subject.

So, by an extraordinary chance, it was Tomsk who happened on the guilty secret of Bungo and Alderney. For Tomsk had become rather bored with just doing exercises hour after hour, and as no Wombles were going out to work on the Common he hadn't got to do any door-keeping, so he was rather at a loose end. Golf was out, of course, as everything was covered in snow, so Tomsk went along to have a look at Tobermory's small library of technical books, and it was there under 'sports' that he came across *Skiing*.

Tomsk was a slow, but deliberate reader, and after a few hours he began to understand what the book was all about. Skiing sounded rather good fun, so Tomsk went back to the Workshop to ask for two long pieces of wood.

Tobermory was very busy in his back office working on whatever-it-was and merely shouted to Tomsk to take what he wanted. Tomsk had a good look round, and finally chose two long pieces of sapling which seemed to resemble the pictures in the book. He had a long and rather painful afternoon trying to get the wood into shape, during which he managed to hammer all his paws, but at the finish he was quite satisfied and rather surprised at what he had managed to achieve. He went to bed with a happy smile on his face and never noticed the rather guilty-yet-smug expression on Bungo's.

It snowed again during the night, and when Tomsk left the burrow it was to see a world which was white and sparkling and quite untouched by either Human or Womble paw. The only marks on the gleaming, glittering surface were the claw-marks of the birds, who were having a hard time of it searching for food.

Tomsk tucked his home-made skis under his arm and made for the steepest, least wooded slope he could remember. It was a really beautiful morning, with the sun just up and the snow almost blindingly white except where it was in the shadows, where it turned to deep blue.

Tomsk fitted on his skis, with his tongue caught between his teeth and, remembering all that he had read in the little book, he pushed himself off down the slope. It was a glorious, most wonderful feeling—like running, like jumping, like flying— and Tomsk, who although he was not very clever, and who took half an hour to read a page of print, was a born athlete. He shot down that slope with a marvellous *shushing* sound, and braked at the bottom with no trouble at all, sending up a dazzling fan shape of snow crystals as he did so.

Tomsk was breathless with the wonder of it all, and after three more runs, each better than the last, he decided to have a go at something even more adventurous, so he pushed himself off across the Common, bending low over his skis in exactly the same way as the picture of the Human Being in the book. There was not a soul in sight so there was nothing to worry about and Tomsk hummed between his teeth in a tuneless sort of way as he travelled.

Since the affair of the toppling tree he had been treated with far more respect than ever before in his life, but all the same respect isn't everything, and he still felt lonely sometimes. But now he had discovered something at which he knew instinctively he really was rather good, and at the back of his mind he couldn't help wishing that there was another Womble there to watch him.

Tomsk reached the steepest slope of all, checked that his home-made skis were tightly fastened, took a deep breath and pushed himself off. Oh, what a satisfying sound it was to hear the *shush shush* of his skis over the crisp, unbroken snow! How wonderful to feel the icy cold air against his fur and to narrow his eyes against the dazzle of the rising sun! How glorious to track his path down this steep, steep slope, and how sad there was nobody there to see him.

But there was!

For there, fast appearing out of the blue shadows was someone who Tomsk very much wanted to impress. Great Uncle Bulgaria himself! There he stood at the bottom of the slope wearing his two pairs of spectacles, and his tartan shawl, and with *The Times* under his arm.

'Look at me,' shouted Tomsk, bending his knees in an expert fashion and hunching over his skis. Great Uncle Bulgaria watched him with an expressionless face, but Tomsk was too excited to notice. In fact, he was showing off dreadfully, taking his turns too tightly and sending up far too much icy spray as he hurtled down the slope faster and FASTER and FASTER. Indeed too fast, for at the last bend he missed his timing altogether and to Tomsk's horror he suddenly realised that he was heading straight for Great Uncle Bulgaria and that he COULD NOT STOP!

'Look out, look out,' howled Tomsk, and shut his eyes and bent down double. But still Great Uncle Bulgaria refused to move, and the next moment Tomsk hit him, travelling at at least thirty miles an hour.

There was a tremendous THUD, BANG, CRASH, and then Tomsk was going head over heels and Great Uncle Bulgaria had dissolved into a thousand pieces. Tomsk dug himself painfully out of the snow, shook his head and got to his knees, his eyes round as buttons as he stared horror-struck at a tartan shawl, two pairs of spectacles and *The Times* newspaper—and nothing else! Poor Tomsk went as near green as a Womble can and got very shakily to his back paws.

He felt awful. Worse than awful, dreadful. His strong legs would hardly support him as he crawled up the snowy slope. But search though he might he could find no trace of the Oldest Womble but his belongings, which he gathered together with trembling and gentle paws.

Tomsk never knew how he managed to get back to the burrow. It was sheer will-power and muscle-power that did it, and he crawled through the main door with his awful burden (the shawl, spectacles and newspaper) and on trembling paws made his way towards the Workshop. He was just passing the door of Great Uncle Bulgaria's room when—oh horror—it swung slowly open!

Tomsk stopped dead in his tracks with his eyes bulging, as from inside the room there came the sound of shuffling footsteps, and then the door swung wider still and Great Uncle Bulgaria himself came into view.

'*Eeeeeeee*,' whispered Tomsk, and fainted dead away.

'I see,' said Great Uncle Bulgaria some while later, 'so you went right through me, eh? *Most* interesting. *Most* illuminating.'

'I didn't mean to do it,' Tomsk said huskily.

'There, there, I'm sure you didn't,' said Great Uncle Bulgaria in a soothing voice. 'Just you have a nice sip of blackcurrant juice and leave the rest to me, my boy,' and the old Womble shuffled back to his own room and spread his paws to the electric fire and pursed up his lips and looked extremely thoughtful. And then after a while he began to smile, and if any young Womble had seen that expression he might well have had cause to feel very, very worried.

The following morning Bungo got up with a very light heart indeed and straight after breakfast he went round to see Alderney in the kitchen, and even helped her with the washing-up, which made

Madame Cholet rather thoughtful.

'Can I go out now?' said Alderney, with such an innocent look.

'But it has snowed again, my little one,' said Madame Cholet, who didn't care for the cold weather herself.

'That's why,' said Alderney. 'Bungo and me want to have a snowball fight.'

'Very well,' said Madame Cholet, and shrugged and returned to her cooking. So Bungo and Alderney, giggling and whispering, went off to get some boots and scarves and were soon clattering down the passages to the main door where Orinoco was sitting in for Tomsk.

'Off sick,' said Orinoco, who was peeling an orange, 'crashed or something yesterday while he was skiing. Nothing serious.'

Bungo and Alderney went out into the sunshine, which seemed twice as bright because of the glitter of the blinding white snow, and left a small double trail of pawmarks behind them. The sun was so clear it had melted some of the icicles which hung from the trees and every now and again they would slide downwards or start dripping on the bare branches. But Bungo and Alderney were too wrapped up in their own affairs to notice, and they went sliding and slithering across the snow until they reached the top of the steepest slope.

'There it is,' said Bungo, pointing.

'Isn't it splendid,' said Alderney, her head on one side. 'It must be the best snow Womble in the whole world.'

And it did look very lifelike as it stood at the bottom of the hill, with its white arms spread wide and its two pairs of spectacles and its tartan shawl.

There was even a copy of *The Times* propped up beside it.

'I think the ears have melted a bit,' said Bungo, studying his masterpiece.

'And the nose has squashed in,' said Alderney.

'Let's go and build it up again,' said Bungo, and he set off sliding and slithering down the slope, with Alderney right behind him.

'Oh, it is good,' said Bungo, stopping just short of the snow Womble. '*I* don't see what's wrong with making it. If you ask me the older Wombles are a lot too careful.'

And Bungo scooped up a pawful of soft white snow and was about to add it to his snow Womble when quite suddenly out of the middle of nowhere he got the most awful box on the ears.

'Who did that?' cried Bungo, spinning round on his heels.

'I did,' said a dreadful voice. 'So my ears are melting, are they? So my nose is squashed in, is it? So I'm too careful, am I? Take that, young Womble, and that and that and THAT!'

And a perfect hail of snowballs shot past the ears of both Bungo and Alderney. For one moment they stood motionless, looking with horrified and staring eyes at their Womble snow figure which had so awfully come to life, and then with one accord they took to their paws and ran. They ran as they had never run before in their lives and they didn't pause for breath until they were safe and sound inside the burrow again.

'Dear, dear,' said Madame Cholet, when Alderney poured out the story to her.

'*Tsk, tsk, tsk,*' said Tobermory, when Bungo stuttered out his tale of the snow Womble which

96

had come to life.

'Ho-hum,' said Great Uncle Bulgaria. 'Well, well, well. Perhaps this will teach you both to listen to your elders and betters who are a great deal wiser than you are!' And he wriggled his paws in their fur-lined boots.

Standing about on a snow-covered Common at eight in the morning can be very hard on the paws of an old white Womble . . .

CHAPTER 9

ORINOCO AND THE CHOCOLATE CAKE

Rather to Great Uncle Bulgaria's surprise it went on snowing day after day, and the fine white flakes drifting down out of a lead-coloured sky turned the Common into an enchanted land of grand beauty. The leaves of the evergreens looked as if they had been frosted with diamond dust. The tiny waterfalls that usually found their trickling way down to the Queen's Mere were frozen in their tracks and hung suspended in a thousand glass icicles which glittered when the sun sometimes found its way through the grey clouds. Every bare branch was covered in a thick white coat, and when the snow grew too heavy for the trees to carry, there would be a crackling sound and a small avalanche would slither softly to the ground.

The great white blanket covered everything and made it look quite different and feel quite different and sound quite different. The Common grew so quiet the Wombles could hear the ducks skidding and squawking as they tried to land on the Mere, which was now one great snow-speckled mirror, frozen so deep that the fish were trapped in blocks of ice. Every whisper, every snapping of a twig carried through the cold still air.

All the younger Wombles (except for Tomsk who had gone right off skiing) were absolutely delighted with the snow. They had snowball fights and built snow huts, and Tobermory, who had time on his paws at the moment because of the weather, made them some toboggans, and they went careering down the slopes squealing and laughing and quite often falling off and rolling over and over until they looked like fat white snowballs themselves. Tomsk, however, was not very happy. He missed playing golf dreadfully and tobogganing seemed dull after skiing. But on the other hand nothing would ever induce him to ski again. So one way and another Tomsk was rather out of sorts.

'It gets boring doing exercises all the time,' he complained in his slow way to Tobermory. Tobermory scratched his ear with his screwdriver and then went off to the Womble library and searched through the books until he found one called *Tarzan of the Apes*. He handed that over to Tomsk and told him very firmly to read it.

'And no skipping, mind,' said Tobermory, and returned to his toboggan-making.

Tomsk wasn't very good at reading, but he was just a little in awe of Tobermory, so he did what he was told, saying each word aloud to himself under his breath as he went along, and as it was a very good story, he quite enjoyed it in spite of the effort involved.

'Well?' said Tobermory, when Tomsk returned the book.

'It's all about this Human Being who thinks he's a monkey,' said Tomsk. 'He has lots of adventures and he swings through the trees by his paws. He's terribly good at it. I wish *I* could do it.'

'Why don't you try, then?' said Tobermory patiently. Tomsk thought it over for several minutes and then nodded and went off leaving Tobermory chuckling to himself. Tomsk was a very good tree climber—he always won when they played Wombles and Ladders—but he wasn't much good at pretending to be a monkey. However, it was wonderful exercise and although he fell down more times than he swung from branch to branch he didn't hurt himself, because he always landed in a soft bed of snow; and his temper improved no end.

Orinoco enjoyed the snow for quite a different reason. It meant that there was very little work to be done, so he carefully built himself a kind of snow sofa with curves and bumps in just the right places to fit his figure. Then he lined it with dried bracken from one of the store cupboards, borrowed a pair of sunglasses from Tobermory's collection—and a very wide selection there was from which to choose, as Human Beings are better at losing sunglasses than practically anything else except perhaps gloves—and settled himself down for a really long rest with his favourite book from the library. It was called:

FORTUNE & BASON
SPLENDID CHRISTMAS CATALOGUE, 1932

And Bungo and Alderney, of course, were having the time of their lives, although neither of them ever mentioned the idea of building another snow Womble. So all the young ones were extremely happy and contented with this wonderful weather. But with the older Wombles it was quite a different story.

'How much is left in the larders?' asked Great Uncle Bulgaria, when Madame Cholet brought him his mid-morning hot drink. Alderney was out building an igloo, so Madame Cholet was on trolley duty.

'Alas,' said Madame Cholet, 'we are getting low on food.'

'How low?' asked Great Uncle Bulgaria, giving her a sharp look. 'I want the truth now, my good Womble.'

Madame Cholet twisted her apron between her paws and said in a low voice, 'There is enough to last for another ten days. That is all.'

Great Uncle Bulgaria grunted and went over to the barometer which Tobermory had hung on the wall during the Great Rains. He tapped the glass, but the needle stayed firmly at 'Snow'.

'*Tsk, tsk, tsk*,' said Great Uncle Bulgaria, and pushed aside the plans for the great Midsummer outing on which he had been working. The party seemed a long way off at the moment, and his instinct told him that a danger even worse than the floods lay ahead.

A really long hard winter makes life a difficult business for all wild creatures, and the Wombles were no exception, although they were more efficient than most at surviving because they are by nature so thrifty. While the squirrels only stored nuts, the Wombles packed away everything they possibly could. All through the spring, summer and autumn months Madame Cholet was bottling, drying and stacking everything on which she could lay her paws. Nothing was wasted in her kitchen, not a blade of grass or a single berry, not a mushroom stalk or half a bar of chocolate.

Many of the Human Beings who picnicked on the Common would have been astonished to know that what they left behind so untidily was carefully taken back to Madame Cholet, cleaned by washing or boiling, and turned into some delicious dish. Orinoco had been known to track a likely looking picnic party from one side of the Common to the other and no Womble would ever forget the time when he had returned in triumph with a whole bag of perfectly good bananas. Rolled and coated in grass-seed dough they had been baked very slowly and served with thick, creamy rowan berry sauce. It had been one of Madame Cholet's greatest triumphs.

All this went through Great Uncle Bulgaria's mind now, and it made his mouth water. He pushed the memory to one side and said, 'I'd better come and have a look.'

'Very well,' said Madame Cholet rather crossly, for like all good cooks she didn't care for anybody inspecting her kitchens and larders.

Great Uncle Bulgaria's heart sank as they moved through the storerooms. There were all too few full jars, sacks and packets left.

'There's only one thing for it,' he said. 'We'll have to start rationing food. We did it in the bad winter of '46 to '47 and we'll have to do it again. Please fetch Tobermory and we'll work out a scheme together.'

And so the three Wombles sat down at the scrubbed wooden table made from orange boxes, and with papers and pencils and much 'ho-humming' from Great Uncle Bulgaria and sniffs from Madame Cholet they drew up a list of food and a list of Wombles and divided one with the other.

'Perhaps the younger ones should have a little more,' suggested Madame Cholet, who in that family of kindly creatures probably had the warmest heart of all.

That meant a lot more adding and dividing and subtracting and even so it was plain that there would be only enough food to last three weeks and Great Uncle Bulgaria, who could remember one winter when the snow and frost had stayed on the ground for two months, shook his white head, but kept his thoughts to himself.

'If only there was some better way of keeping food,' said Tobermory, sharpening their pencils with the small knife attached to his screwdriver—it was his own invention and a very useful one.

'I'm sure I do my best,' said Madame Cholet, sitting up very straight.

'Yes, yes, of course,' said Tobermory hastily, 'only there are times such as September when we have a glut of blackberries and mushrooms . . .'

'. . . and toadstools,' put in Great Uncle Bulgaria, who had a weakness for this delicacy, which is poisonous to Human Beings but much enjoyed by Wombles, some of whom are convinced that it prevents falling fur.

'Yes,' agreed Madame Cholet reluctantly, 'but I bottle all I can, and mushrooms and toadstools just *will* not keep. They go wormy.'

'Exactly what I mean,' said Tobermory. 'Just think how splendid it would be if we had some *now*.'

All three Wombles licked their lips and sighed and then pulled themselves together.

'*If wishes were wings then Wombles would fly,*' said Great Uncle Bulgaria, quoting an old proverb. 'Rationing must start immediately, Madame Cholet. I shall make an announcement in the Common Room *before* lunch.'

The news was greeted by the Wombles in shocked silence, and several of the younger ones wished that they had stopped to eat a larger breakfast instead of rushing off to play in the snow. When they saw their plates their faces fell more than ever, and a kind of gloomy shiver ran through their fur.

'This is simply *dreadful*,' whispered Orinoco, who had worked up a nice appetite from lying in the pale sunlight.

'I don't understand it,' said Alderney, thinking sadly of her little trolley which Madame Cholet had told her would not be used until after the thaw. She did so enjoy pushing it along the corridors and ringing the bell.

'It's quite simple,' said Bungo, who had been listening to the older Wombles and who was getting a little more grown-up every day. 'There are two reasons really. First, Human Beings don't come on to the Common at all when the weather's like this, except if they are exercising their dogs and then, of course, they don't bring any food with them. And second, we can't get at anything that's growing—not that there is much in the winter—

because of the snow.'

'Then how do the birds manage?' asked Alderney.

'Quite often they don't,' said Tobermory, who had overheard this question and who felt that the three young Wombles were now old enough to learn some of the harsher facts of existence. 'They die.'

At this a really dreadful gloom settled on the table and Alderney began to sniff, so to cheer her up Bungo suggested a game of Wombles and Ladders. Alderney soon perked up a bit, but Orinoco became steadily more and more upset. He knew he was greedy, he was perfectly aware that he thought too much about food, and ever since he had got stuck in the rabbit hole he had tried to be better. But now, faced with a real shortage, his whole tubby little body longed and yearned and ached for food. He made matters worse for himself by imagining all his favourite menus, from bracken and berry pie to chocolate and orange-skin cake. Every night he had wonderful dreams in which by some miracle Madame Cholet suddenly discovered a forgotten larder and dished up the most enormous high tea.

Poor Orinoco would wake up groaning and with his tongue hanging out, and in spite of all Great Uncle Bulgaria's instructions he would slip along the silent passages, past the other slumbering Wombles and down to the small back door near the road to see if it had stopped snowing yet.

But each time all he saw were the soft, shining flakes filtering slowly on to the Common and the rooftops. It had even hardened on the road so that the traffic moved far more slowly than usual, and

at all times of the day and night there were Human
Beings throwing shovel-loads of yellow sand on it
to make it less slippery. The sand made Orinoco
think of lovely fine yellow sugar, and he groaned
more than ever.

And every day the Wombles grew a little thinner
and their fur became a little less sleek and their
eyes more worried.

'Perhaps we could buy some food,' suggested
Tobermory.

'We've got very little English money left,'
replied Great Uncle Bulgaria, who was becoming a
shadow of his former self for, unknown to anyone
but Madame Cholet, the old Womble had cut his
own rations in half and insisted that the rest should
be divided among the younger ones. 'When you
get to my age you don't need so much,' he said,
pulling his tartan shawl more closely round his
shoulders so that she shouldn't notice how straggly
his white fur had become.

'We should never have bought all that concrete,' said Tobermory. 'It was my fault, worrying on about foundations and cracks. You reminded me once that Wombles were more important than mere things. You were right.'

'Don't be an idiot,' said Great Uncle Bulgaria, who hated seeing his usually strong-minded friend showing such weakness. 'We couldn't have foreseen this snow siege. If things do get really bad then we'll be forced to buy—but it'll only mean about one biscuit each. I'm going to read *The Times*. Think I'll have a copy of the Jubilee Summer in 1935. I remember that I never did finish that crossword.'

It was on the nineteenth day of rationing that Orinoco was woken up by the sound of his own empty stomach rumbling. He had been dreaming of fungus tarts, and for a moment the reality of there being no such things available was almost more than he could bear. He shook his head and clambered out of bed and tiptoed past Bungo and went off down the long dark passage.

Surely, surely, it would have stopped snowing by now? But it hadn't. Little drifts of white flakes flurried into his face and settled on his fur. Orinoco blinked his eyes and made a sound which was almost a sob. He was so upset that for a minute or two he didn't realise that something unusual was happening by the flashing lights of the black and white crossing. Then it did slowly occur to him that there was a great deal of activity for one o'clock in the morning, so he edged towards the snowy bushes to investigate.

It appeared that not quite enough sand had been put down, or perhaps the deep cold had turned the road to ice, for there, tipped up against a tree, was a large van. Two of its wheels were stuck up in the air, its back doors had swung open and a group of Human Beings were standing round arguing and talking and stamping their feet.

Orinoco moved a little closer, keeping in the shadows, and then, almost unbelievingly, he saw that a large crate had fallen out of the van and was lying on the snow with half its contents spilled about it.

'Cakes,' breathed Orinoco, rubbing his paws in his eyes the better to see this glorious sight. 'Buns, rolls, bread!'

The food was already being covered with a thin layer of snow and it was icy cold, but even so the delicious smell of newly baked food swam round Orinoco's nose. And what was more the food was lying ON THE COMMON, and Orinoco knew that no Human Being would salvage it once it had been spilled on the ground.

Orinoco registered all this in a flash and then with one excited whimper, he burrowed through the bushes, grasped the crate with one paw and shovelled everything back into it with the other. A pick-up van with a flashing yellow light on the roof was slowly coming down the road, and the Human Beings were far too interested in that to notice one desperate Womble tugging a large box into the bushes.

Although it was as large as he was Orinoco pushed and pulled, pulled and pushed that beautiful heavy crate all the way to the back door of the burrow without stopping for a rest. Then he leant against the wall and with his tongue hanging out and his breath coming in excited gasps he investigated his discovery.

It was glorious, astonishing, absolutely fantastic. The rich spicy smell made his heart whirl and his stomach rumble even louder than before. For one second Orinoco hesitated and then before he could control his paws they had picked up a particularly succulent chocolate cake and rammed it into his open mouth.

Orinoco didn't bother to chew it at all, he was too anxious to get at a lovely sticky Chelsea bun and then a sausage roll. It was when he tasted the meat that his wild delirium was halted, for Wombles are not carnivorous. So he spat out the sausage and buried it in the snow, and then shut his eyes as shame flooded over him. He had been taught all his life that Wombles shared everything. It was true that there were some private possessions such as Tobermory's screwdriver and Great Uncle Bulgaria's tartan shawl, but these were really only on loan.

What Orinoco had just done was an almost unforgivable crime, for while the other Wombles were starving—and they were very close to it by now—he, Orinoco, had stuffed himself.

'Ohhhhhhh,' groaned Orinoco, wringing his paws.

He was not a particularly brave Womble, but he knew at this moment that the only thing he could possibly do was to go to Great Uncle Bulgaria and tell him everything. Orinoco took a deep breath and opened his eyes and picked up the crate and at the very same moment a terrible voice said in his ear, 'You wicked, *wicked* Womble.'

It was Tobermory, who had been wandering about trying to discover where the cold draught was coming from, for Orinoco had forgotten to shut the door behind himself.

'I was just going to take this to Great Uncle Bulgaria,' whispered Orinoco.

'*After* you have gorged your own miserable stomach,' said Tobermory, still in the same dreadful voice, which made Orinoco shake to his back paws.

'How—how did you know?' asked Orinoco, in a mere thread of a voice.

'Chocolate crumbs on your whiskers,' said Tobermory, and he shut the door and bolted it and folded his arms while Orinoco went scuttling off down the passage making a terrified little whimpering noise.

CHAPTER 10

BUNGO'S GREAT ADVENTURE

What was said at that meeting in the middle of the night none of the other Wombles ever discovered and they were far too polite to ask. Of course the general gist of it leaked out, and there was a great deal of shocked whispering in corners, especially when Great Uncle Bulgaria stumped into breakfast with his white fur looking quite lank and dull and his back more bowed than anyone had ever seen it before. And when a squabble broke out at one of the lower tables between two young Wombles over who should have an apple core, Great Uncle Bulgaria didn't even put on his staring spectacles. He just looked at them in such a sad way that it struck terror into their small hearts, and their fur rose up in prickles and they didn't utter another sound until the end of the meal.

The truth was that Great Uncle Bulgaria hadn't

even noticed the noise particularly; his mind was on other things. He felt that he had failed. Failed to teach the Wombles properly and, even worse, failed in his trust to guard and look after them. He should have foreseen this dreadful winter, and somehow made provision for it, but now it was too late.

And as for Orinoco, he was sitting on his bed with his front paws clutched between his knees and his eyes fixed on the wall. He was, without doubt, the most miserable Womble in the whole world. He felt lower than the lowest worm and as he was normally rather fond of himself this was a terrible sensation.

'I'm a wicked, wicked Womble,' he whispered, rocking backwards and forwards.

It was true that he, and he alone, had brought in enough food to last one more day, but that didn't seem to make things much better at the moment. In fact, Orinoco for the first time in his happy-go-lucky existence was struggling with the pangs of a truly dreadful remorse. He was, of course, painting matters much blacker than they really were, for the Wombles are a kindly lot and in a matter of days Great Uncle Bulgaria and Tobermory would have forgiven him. But Orinoco was quite unable to look that far ahead, and he couldn't bear the thought of being despised.

Suddenly an idea came into his head. He would run away. With him gone there would at least be his ration of food to be divided amongst the others, and that would more than make up for what he had stuffed into his greedy mouth that morning.

To think was to act. Orinoco scribbled a note

112

and pinned it to his pillow; then he put on his battered straw hat and tied the scarf over it and wound it round his neck and across his chest and knotted it at the back. He gave one last look round the room and then very quietly let himself out and tiptoed along the empty passage.

It was still snowing, although not so hard, and Orinoco felt rather sad, yet noble and brave at the same time. He walked quickly, with his head bent against the gusts of wind, and quite soon his small pawmarks were being blown away and then completely blotted out by the drifting, silent snow.

Orinoco's disappearance was not discovered until the early afternoon. Everybody felt that he would rather be left alone so they didn't go to his room, but after a while Bungo, who had finished his work in the Workshop, decided to go and have a chat with him.

'Hi, Orinoco, old chap,' he said, putting his head round the door.

Naturally there was no reply and Bungo was about to leave when he noticed the note on the pillow. It was addressed to Great Uncle Bulgaria so he took it to him immediately. The old Womble was dozing in front of the fire, *The Times* spread across his lap. He read the note and sat up with a thump, his paws trembling.

'Fetch Tobermory,' he snapped.

Tobermory came at once, still carrying a steering wheel which he had been straightening.

'Read this. Read it aloud. Bungo, listen,' commanded Great Uncle Bulgaria.

'*Dear Great Uncle Bulgaria, I have gone to seek*

my fortune. I am only a disapointment . . . That should have two p's,' said Tobermory.

'Go on, go on,' said Great Uncle Bulgaria, thumping the floor with his stick.

'*A disapointment and a trial to you. I once hid a bottle of lemonade and some other food too, but I never ate it. Bungo knows about it. Please share my rations with everybody else, particularly Bungo if possible. Yours very respectfully, Orinoco Womble. P.S. Have taken the hat and scarf, hope you don't mind. P.P.S. Hope that the Midsummer party is great fun and you have lots to eat. O.W.*'

'Well,' said Tobermory and blew his nose violently on a large purple handkerchief.

Bungo didn't say anything at all, he just stood there with his mouth hanging open.

'Young fool,' said Great Uncle Bulgaria, who suddenly looked much more his old self, for there's nothing like worrying about somebody else's troubles to make you forget your own. 'Idiot, noddle-top, *cork-brain*, addle-pate, THICKHEAD.'

And he got up and began to pace backwards and forwards across the room talking all the time. 'Of course we'll have to bring him back. Why, a Womble hasn't been lost from this Common since the great kidnapping in 1914—or was it '15? Still that's beside the point, and anyway I wasn't in control then. But I am *now* and I'm not going to have it. Do you understand!' And he suddenly turned on Bungo, who nearly jumped out of his fur.

'Yes, I mean, no,' said Bungo.

'You're a fool too,' said Great Uncle Bulgaria. 'Knew you were a fool when you chose a name like Bungo. Silly sort of name. Still you've improved a bit recently, I'll say that for you,' and he shot a shrewd look at Bungo as though he were weighing something up in his mind. 'Well then, seeing that you're a friend of Orinoco's, where do you think he's run to? Eh?'

'I can't imagine,' said Bungo wretchedly. 'He always seemed so happy here.'

There was a short worried silence and then Tobermory said suddenly, 'Wait! There was a book he was always getting out of the library . . .' And with a speed surprising in a Womble of his age he left the room, to return three minutes later with a large and somewhat tattered catalogue. It was extremely brightly coloured and printed in gold across the front were the words:

FORTUNE & BASON
SPLENDID CHRISTMAS CATALOGUE, 1932

'Don't see why this should interest Orinoco,' muttered Great Uncle Bulgaria, flipping through the pages which showed pictures of clothes and jewellery. 'Ho-hum. Ah yes, yes indeed. *Now* we're getting somewhere.' And he thrust the booklet under Tobermory's nose.

'Cream Chocolate Raspberry Truffles, our speciality,' read out Tobermory. 'Fifty pence a pound. Whipped Coconut Icing Dollops. Rare Rich Pomegranates in thick Hungarian honey. Turkish Coffee Fudge. Sugar-coated Chocolate Mice . . . dear me! It all sounds most indigestible.'

'Daresay it does,' agreed Great Uncle Bulgaria. 'But just the sort of thing to take Orinoco's fancy all the same. That's where he's gone, to Fortune and Bason in Piccadilly. Someone will have to go after him!'

'Who?' said Bungo.

The two old Wombles said nothing, but they glanced at each other and then fixed their eyes on Bungo in a most unnerving way.

'Tomsk is larger,' murmured Tobermory, 'but . . .'

'Ho-hum, quite,' agreed Great Uncle Bulgaria, 'but this young Womble on the other hand . . .'

'It's a possibility,' agreed Tobermory.

'What is, please?' asked Bungo, unable to keep quiet any longer.

'You are,' said Great Uncle Bulgaria, suddenly making up his mind. 'You are, young Bungo. You'll have to go after Orinoco and bring him home.'

'M-m-me?' said Bungo. 'But, but, but, but . . .'

'You've got *some* brains when you care to use 'em,' said Great Uncle Bulgaria, 'and you're strong and healthy *and* you're Orinoco's best friend. Tobermory—the map of London, the Underground map, something warm to wear, and what money we can spare.'

'At once,' said Tobermory, and was out of the room before he'd finished speaking. Bungo, for once, didn't say a word, but continued to stand and stare silently at Great Uncle Bulgaria, who was rocking backwards and forwards very fast.

'You've only been off the Common three times,' said Great Uncle Bulgaria. 'Twice to the building site and once when you took Mr D. Smith home, so this'll be a great adventure for you. Here's some good advice, so listen carefully. One: don't speak to more Human Beings than you have to. The chances are they'll never notice you're a Womble, but there's no necessity to take risks. Two: take things slowly. Don't rush round in circles and get in a panic. Three: count your change carefully. Four: don't argue with Orinoco. Tell him he's to come back with you and that's an order from ME. Five: should anything go very wrong then you may ask a policeman for help. Six: remember your manners. Seven: always look both ways before crossing a road. Got all that?'

'Yes,' said Bungo, whose head was spinning. He went rapidly through Great Uncle Bulgaria's good advice in his mind, and had just reached number seven when Tobermory came back into the room laden with objects.

'Flat cap, one,' he said, starting to lay the things down in a neat pile. 'Sheepskin coat, fully lined—lovely piece of material—mittens and boots ditto. Twenty-five pence, please count it. Map of the Underground, one. Large map of London, one.'

'Give it here,' said Great Uncle Bulgaria.

They spread the map out on the floor and the old Womble pointed out the Common with his stick while Bungo watched him, his heart pounding furiously with excitement.

'That's us,' said Great Uncle Bulgaria. 'You will proceed . . .'

Bungo glanced at Tobermory who whispered, 'He means walk.'

'Proceed,' said Great Uncle Bulgaria with a quelling look, 'across the Common in a south-easterly direction, crossing the road at the building site. You will then go due south until you reach the High Street. Follow this road until you come to Wimbledon Station. See, there, that red circle.'

'Um, um,' said Bungo, nodding.

'Where you will catch a District Line train to Earls Court Station. There. It's the only train you *can* catch as it happens, so you shouldn't find it too difficult. At Earls Court you will change trains and take the Piccadilly Line to Piccadilly Circus. There. See, it's marked in blue.'

'Um, um.'

'You will get out at Piccadilly Circus and walk down Piccadilly until you see Fortune and Bason on your left-paw side. There you will find Orinoco. Now, please repeat your instructions.'

'Oh my, oh my,' muttered Bungo to himself, and then in a somewhat hoarse voice he did as he was asked with hardly a stumble.

'Not bad, not bad,' said Great Uncle Bulgaria. 'You will take the Underground map with you in your pocket. Now then, put on your clothes and count your money.'

Bungo could hardly dress himself he was shaking so much, and the sheepskin coat was so hot he had to start panting.

'You'll do,' said Great Uncle Bulgaria as Bungo slowly turned round. He got stiffly to his feet and put out his snow-white paw. 'Good luck, young Womble. This is the greatest adventure of your life, and also the most important and *responsible* thing you've ever had to do. I'm depending on you to do it properly, and what's more,' added Great Uncle Bulgaria with rather less solemnity, 'you can tell Orinoco from me not to be more of a fool than he can help.'

'Um, um,' said Bungo.

He marched out a little stiffly, owing to the boots, and Great Uncle Bulgaria sat down again and shook his head and then glanced at Tobermory.

'Do you think he will be able to manage?' he

118

asked in a low voice. 'After all, he's never been into London proper on his own before.'

'Of course he will,' said Tobermory gruffly. 'Grown up a lot lately, Bungo has. Noticed it several times. I'll just see him off.'

And he hurried after Bungo and caught him up by the back door of the burrow.

'Steady up, young Womble,' Tobermory said. 'Got a little bit more for you here.' And from his large apron pocket he produced a compass, half a bar of chocolate and a tidy-bag. '*That's* to make sure you're going in the right direction, that's to keep you going, and this is for just in case you happen to see anything in the food line along the way.'

And Tobermory put his paw on Bungo's shoulder for a moment and then opened the door on to the outside world. If he hadn't been in such a state Bungo might have noticed that it had actually stopped snowing and that the air was just that little bit warmer. However, his mind was firmly fixed on trying to remember all Great Uncle Bulgaria's instructions, and as he crunched (rather flat-footedly) through the snow, he kept repeating them under his breath. It was of course, an enormous honour to be trusted with the quest for Orinoco and it made him feel proud, frightened and anxious by turns. He found the black and white path, consulted the compass and set off down the deserted pavement.

It was quite a long walk to get to the Underground station, but he passed very few people for it was a nasty afternoon and the ground was extremely slippery. Bungo paid for his ticket and the inspector at the gate hardly glanced at him as he marched past and down on to the platform. However, when the train came roaring and rattling towards him, for two pins he would have turned and run for it. The only thing that stopped him was the fact that he was a great deal more scared of what Great Uncle Bulgaria and Tobermory would say to him if he did go back.

The carriage was nearly empty and Bungo sat huddled up at one end, counting the stations, reading his map and saying over and over to himself: 'Change at Earls Court on to the Piccadilly Line. Change at Earls Court . . .'

Which, as it turned out, was a great deal easier said than done, for Earl's Court Station was full of people shoving and pushing and Bungo nearly got swept backwards into the carriage which he was trying rather timidly to leave. So he had to forget his usual good manners and he shoved and pushed with everybody else and somehow he managed to find the right train. And then he was off again, wedged up against the doors by a very fat Human Being who was reading an evening paper. Bungo read the headlines which said, 'Thaw Coming', but he didn't take the words in at all and only wondered briefly who Thaw could be. And then he forgot all about it as he saw a thin woman quite deliberately push a paper bag with half a loaf in it down the side of the seat.

'Fantastic,' muttered Bungo and edged over, and when she got out at Green Park he picked up the bag and put it into his tidy-bag. By the time he got to Piccadilly he had also acquired a pair of gloves, a scarf, a baby's rattle and a copy of that morning's *Times*, which he knew Great Uncle Bulgaria would be delighted to have.

Bungo was so overcome by all this untidiness that he nearly missed Piccadilly altogether and if he hadn't lost so much weight recently he would have been nipped by the doors as they slid shut.

The escalator was a bit of a worry and Bungo travelled up with his eyes fixed to the ground, as he was frightened he would be swept away and down a crack if he didn't watch out. It was very hot in the Underground and what with his sheepskin coat and his own fur Bungo was very warm indeed, but he knew he was far safer if he stayed dressed up like everybody else, so he just put out his tongue and panted. It was a relief to discover that, as Great Uncle Bulgaria had predicted, the Human Beings all about him took no notice of the fact that he was a Womble. They were all far too busy about their own affairs and Bungo, who had never before been so close to so many people, decided that beside being dreadfully wasteful they were also remarkably unobservant.

'Funny creatures,' he muttered to himself.

Piccadilly Station is very muddling for those who don't know it and Bungo walked round it three times before he found the right exit. It was wonderful to get out into the air again and he took in several deep breaths and then gulped in astonishment as he looked about him. Bungo was, after all, used to the quiet orderly life of the Common and he had been too young to start working until the autumn so he had never seen his own home territory when it was crowded. He would never have believed that there were so many Human Beings in the world. Or so many cars and vans and lorries and taxis and buses. Or such bright lights, for all about him there were enormous brilliantly coloured signs, blinking on and off, making patterns and forming pictures. Bungo turned round and round with his head back and his mouth wide open.

This would indeed be something to tell the other Wombles. Only how could he ever describe it to them? It was like nothing he had ever imagined, not even from the books in the library. Added to which there was such a tremendous noise.

'Mind where you're going, can't you?' shouted somebody, almost pushing the slowly revolving Bungo off the pavement and in front of a Number 19 bus. That brought him back to his senses and he swallowed and took a grip on himself, consulted the map and the compass and began to walk slowly along Piccadilly, searching for Fortune and Bason. There were a number of brightly coloured shops, and when Bungo saw food in one of the windows he just couldn't help stopping for a moment. There was a box of chocolates as large as a bicycle wheel and dozens of boxes of other sweets as well as little pyramids of nougat and fudge and Turkish delight and sugared almonds and candied fruits and toffees and mints and liquorice and chocolate drops and rows and rows of bottles of boiled sweets.

Unlike Orinoco Bungo hadn't got a very sweet tooth, but on the other hand he hadn't had much to eat for nearly three weeks and his knees went weak at the sight of all this delicious, chewy, melting goodness.

It also made him think of Orinoco, and he leant against the brightly lit glass for a moment and tried to control a sudden rush of hunger, homesickness and fright at the enormity of his quest and the

122

terror of this great adventure. How could he possibly hope to find his friend in this large, noisy, hurrying, bad-tempered crowd of Human Beings?

With trembling paws Bungo took out his half bar of chocolate and ate it slowly to recover his nerve. He was made of stern stuff and he had been well taught by Great Uncle Bulgaria, but he was also one small, almost lost Womble in the centre of a teeming, uncaring city. Excitement had carried him along this far, but the sight of all that food had weakened him and also dulled his instincts, which should have warned him that for the last hundred yards he had been followed!

'Come on,' Bungo whispered to himself. 'Are you a Womble or a mouse?'

He straightened his shoulders and marched on, the tidy-bag banging against his side. The snow had been swept off the pavements and piled into dirty grey banks on the kerb, and every now and again Bungo got pushed into the slush, and once he was showered with wet, sticky mush by a bus as it went roaring past.

Bungo's head began to spin and there's no doubt that he was more than a little light-headed when at last he saw before him the elegant shape of Fortune and Bason. There was food in the windows here too, but it was all done up in smart little packets, tins and boxes, and when Bungo actually saw one small carton with the words CREAM CHOCOLATE RASPBERRY TRUFFLES on the side, it was almost like meeting an old friend.

Bungo pressed his nose to the glass for a moment and then moved hesitantly towards the doors, but as he reached them he saw a man in a very smart green uniform bolt them shut from the inside. Fortune and Bason were closing for the night.

'Let me in, let me in,' cried Bungo, knocking frantically on the glass, for he was now convinced that Orinoco must be inside there somewhere, looking for spilt Cream Chocolate Raspberry Truffles or Sugared Mice at the very least. But the man took no notice and at the same moment someone tapped on Bungo's shoulder and a voice said politely in his ear, 'Can I be of any assistance, sir?'

Bungo spun round and found himself face to face with a strange Womble . . .

CHAPTER 11

YELLOWSTONE WOMBLE

Bungo shut his eyes tight and counted up to ten and then opened them again, but the strange Womble was still there watching him with polite interest. He was most beautifully dressed in a narrow brimmed hat of pale grey, a long Crombie overcoat of the same colour, tan gloves and highly polished shoes. He was quite old, for his fur was turning a lovely, silky grey.

'May I introduce myself?' he said, and took a wallet from his pocket and produced a card.

Bungo's paw was shaking so much he nearly dropped it, but he did just manage to make out the words Y. B. WOMBLE, SENIOR. UNITED STATES.

'I beg—I beg your pardon,' said Bungo, raising his cap. The strange Womble lifted his hat and said again, 'Can I be of any assistance, sir?'

'Excuse me,' said Bungo, 'but you are a Womble, aren't you?'

'Yes indeed. Cousin Yellowstone Boston Womble. And you are?'

'Bungo Womble. Of Wimbledon Common. England.'

'Well, bless me,' said Cousin Yellowstone, in exactly the same way as Great Uncle Bulgaria said it. 'If that isn't an astonishing coincidence. I was hoping to visit with you during my stay. But aren't you rather young to be wandering round London on your own?'

These words brought Bungo back to earth and reminded him of his quest. Talking with increasing speed he told Cousin Yellowstone about the reason for his being in Piccadilly, and the difficulties in which he now found himself with Orinoco *inside* Fortune and Bason and himself *outside*.

'Dear, dear me,' said Cousin Yellowstone at the finish of this somewhat rambling story. 'If you'll allow me to make a suggestion, I would guess that your friend Orinoco is also outside. Fortune and Bason are—er—rather narrow-minded about their customers and I do not believe that they would allow a young Womble wearing a straw hat and a scarf to remain inside their portals for long.'

'You mean they'd have thrown him out?' said Bungo in horror.

'Not thrown,' corrected Cousin Yellowstone. 'Escorted with the utmost courtesy and civility.'

'Then what shall I do?' asked Bungo, wringing his paws.

'You say your friend is partial to these candies?' said Cousin Yellowstone thoughtfully. His shrewd eyes had long ago noticed Bungo's thin shape in spite of the sheepskin coat, and he had guessed that he had heard only half the story. In his youth Cousin Yellowstone had journeyed to Canada and experienced the really gruelling fight for survival which went on among all creatures, even man, during those long, frozen winters. He had put two and two together, and because he was a Womble of very wide experience he went on, 'I believe your friend may have gone round the side of this elegant store, to where they nightly put out their so-called trash.'

'Then let us go there immediately,' said Bungo.

'Follow me,' said Cousin Yellowstone, and led the way down a much quieter side street where there were fewer people and less traffic. It was not so brightly lit as the main thoroughfare and as Bungo and Cousin Yellowstone approached the second doorway they saw a small figure crouching in the shadows between two bulging sacks.

'Orinoco!' shouted Bungo, his voice cracking with relief.

Orinoco jumped violently, and then cautiously stepped out into the light. He was a sorry figure. His fur was wet and bedraggled and covered in splashes of melting yellow snow. His straw boater, which had never looked its best since it was soaked in Queen's Mere, was now a shadow of its former self and his scarf had two big holes in it. Orinoco had been on his own in a terrifying city for nearly a whole day, during which time he had been pushed and shoved in all directions. He had walked all the way from Wimbledon and his paws hurt and, because of stubborn pride, he hadn't eaten a mouthful since the two pastries of the early morning. At the sight of Bungo suddenly appearing out of nowhere, Orinoco's mouth twitched and he might have done something as UnWombly as to sniff tearfully if Cousin Yellowstone hadn't said quickly, 'I'm pleased to make your acquaintance, sir,' and held out his paw.

Orinoco shook it, his eyes almost bulging out of his head in a way which suddenly struck Bungo as amazingly funny.

'Good old Orinoco,' he said, buffeting his friend on the shoulder. 'Good, good old Orinoco. Trust you to find out where the food is.'

'I haven't touched a bite,' said Orinoco between stiff lips. 'I was collecting it for—for . . .' His voice trembled.

'Well, my goodness me,' said Cousin Yellowstone. 'Will you just look at that? Why, you must have nearly a sackful there. That's absolutely marvellous. And what fine stuff it is too. I see you have truffles, and what's this? Bless me, candied fruits. Why, I haven't seen them in years. You must have been very, very busy collecting-wise.'

'Gosh,' said Bungo, taking his cue from his American relation. 'I say, Orinoco, you *have* been going at it. Did you do it all by yourself?'

'Um-hum,' said Orinoco, who still wasn't up to saying much.

'Oh, I'm so sorry,' said Bungo, tactfully looking away from his friend's puckered face. 'I haven't introduced you properly. Cousin Yellowstone from America, this is my friend Orinoco from Wimbledon Common.'

'Glad to know you, young Womble,' said Cousin Yellowstone. 'Well, I daresay we should be getting along. I'll call a cab.'

'Can you—I mean, they're rather expensive,' said Bungo.

'Well, I believe I could just about make the fare,' said Cousin Yellowstone. 'You just wait right there.'

The two young Wombles watched his dapper figure disappear out of sight and then Orinoco said in a low voice, 'I don't think I should go back. Not after what happened.'

'I don't know what happened and I don't want to know,' said Bungo, which was noble of him, as he was consumed with curiosity. 'And anyhow if you weren't going to come home, what were you going to do with all that food?'

'Leave it outside the burrow,' said Orinoco. He was feeling a little more like his old self now and he straightened his back as he spoke. 'It *is* rather a good haul, isn't it? I found a perfectly good shopping basket inside a telephone box place. And then I went into Fortune and Bason and . . .' He stopped, and after a moment went on. 'How did you know where to find me anyway?'

'It was Tobermory. He and Great Uncle Bulgaria were awfully upset when they read your letter and they sent me off to find you and here I am.'

'It's jolly good of you,' said Orinoco gruffly.

' 'S all right,' said Bungo, wriggling his paws inside his fur boots. 'Cousin Yellowstone's nice, isn't he?'

'Um,' said Orinoco, nodding violently.

The two young Wombles looked at each other and then looked away, and Orinoco whistled softly and Bungo hummed to himself until a taxi swung round the corner with Cousin Yellowstone leaning out of the window.

'Here, driver,' he said.

The taxi driver looked rather doubtfully at Bungo and Orinoco—who were luckily standing in the shadows—and he frowned even more when Orinoco picked up his very laden shopping basket, and Bungo handed in his carrier on the top of which he had just stuffed three slightly damaged Christmas stockings which he'd noticed sticking out of one of Fortune and Bason's rubbish sacks.

'Wimbledon Common please, driver,' said Cousin Yellowstone.

'Whereabouts on Wimbledon Common, sir?'

'I'll tell you when we get there,' said Cousin Yellowstone firmly and shut the small glass panel so that he and the two young Wombles could talk in private. Actually he did most of the talking himself, as he could see that they were both extremely tired, and long before they reached the suburb of Wimbledon Orinoco was fast asleep with his head, battered straw hat and all, on Bungo's shoulder. Cousin Yellowstone smiled to himself

130

and went on talking softly until Bungo suddenly jerked upright as he recognised the building site and the black and white crossing, which was now perfectly visible as the snow was melting fast.

Cousin Yellowstone knocked on the glass and the taxi stopped and they all climbed out. The driver looked at them, shook his head and only muttered a gruff 'Thanks, guv' when Cousin Yellowstone tipped him most generously.

'No manners, Human Beings,' said Cousin Yellowstone as the taxi drove off through the slush. 'Now then, let me see if I remember the way correctly.'

'You?' said Bungo, with Orinoco echoing him.

'Yes, indeed,' said Cousin Yellowstone. 'I've been here before—once. Long, long ago, before either of you was born. Tell me, is Uncle Bulgaria still reading *The Times* newspaper?'

'Yes,' said Bungo. 'But he's Great Uncle Bulgaria now.'

'Is that right?' said Cousin Yellowstone. 'My, how the years do roll by. Well, shall I lead the way?' And he set off at a brisk pace through the bushes.

Before any of them reached the back door it was thrown open, and Tobermory came out with a lantern held above his head.

'You've taken long enough . . .' he began, and then he saw Cousin Yellowstone and for a moment his eyes bulged just as Orinoco's had done, and he said huskily, 'Why, I do believe—yes, it is! Yellowstone!'

'Tobermory!' exclaimed the American Womble. 'I'd have known you anywhere. Still wearing that apron, I see.'

'Aye,' said Tobermory at his gruffest, 'and by the looks of things you've done well for yourself. So there you are, Orinoco; a nice mess you've made of things to be sure. Come in so I can close the door. The weather's turned, but it's still chilly. Well done, Bungo,' and for a second his grey paw touched Bungo's shoulder, and then he was hurrying off down the passage, blowing out the lantern as he went.

'You'd better go and have something to eat,' Tobermory called over his shoulder. 'Madame Cholet's waiting for you.'

'I've brought some food,' said Orinoco, 'quite a lot of it.'

But Tobermory had already gone on with Cousin Yellowstone, and so the two young Wombles stumbled into the nice bright kitchen where Madame Cholet was stirring something hot and savoury-smelling on the stove, and Alderney was chopping up grass in a very professional manner.

'Well, well, well,' said Madame Cholet, 'take off your wet things and put them there to dry. I never saw such a sorry-looking pair of Wombles in my whole life. Good gracious, what is this?'

For Orinoco had tipped up his shopping basket and the food was spilling across the floor. Bungo added his half loaf and three Christmas stockings and Madame Cholet sat down on the nearest chair and fanned her face and Alderney plumped down on her knees and picked up the pretty packets and paper bags with cries of delight.

'It's to make up for you-know-what,' said Orinoco.

'Is it, indeed?' said Madame Cholet. 'Well,

whatever it may be I'm sure it's all over and done with now. Sit down and have your porridge and then you can tell me about your adventures.'

The adventures lost nothing in the telling and although Wombles don't lie perhaps Bungo and Orinoco did make the most of what had been happening to them.

'Chased you out of the shop!' said Madame Cholet to Orinoco, her eyes wide with horror.

'Well, not *exactly* chased perhaps,' said Orinoco, shifting round on his stool, 'but this Human Being did sort of take hold of my scarf. He was quite polite, but he didn't let go until I was in the street again. He was wearing a coat with tails on it.'

'Tails! Never!' said Madame Cholet, throwing up her paws.

'Tails,' said Orinoco firmly. 'May I scrape out the saucepan, please?'

Which showed that he was fast recovering from all his harrowing experiences—experiences which were at this very moment being recited to Great Uncle Bulgaria by Cousin Yellowstone. The oldest Womble had hardly been able to believe his eyes when that elegant American relation first entered his room. He had got up very slowly from his rocking chair and looked through one pair of spectacles and then the other and then both at once while Tobermory stood smiling in his rather grim way by the door.

'Yellowstone?' said Great Uncle Bulgaria. 'I did hear a rumour many years ago that you might have got to America, but I never knew whether it was true or not.'

'It sure was,' said Cousin Yellowstone. 'My, it's good to see you again, Uncle Bulgaria. Or perhaps

I should say Great Uncle Bulgaria now to avoid confusion. You're just the same.'

'No, I'm not. You're thinking what an old doddery Womble I've become, and in those days my fur was only starting to turn grey. Yours was dark brown I recall. Well, sit down, sit down.'

And he clasped Yellowstone's paw and patted it fiercely before leading him to a chair.

'And now, my dear fellow,' said Great Uncle Bulgaria, 'were you really kidnapped in—er—'14, wasn't it?'

'Spring of '15,' said Yellowstone, holding out his paws to the fire. 'I was a foolish young Womble in those days. Thought I knew everything and the answer to it . . .'

'They all do,' agreed Great Uncle Bulgaria, 'which reminds me, Tobermory, you might tell Bungo and Orinoco that I'd like a word with the pair of them in the morning. So sorry, Yellowstone, pray proceed.'

'It had been a hard winter for us, rather like this one,' said Cousin Yellowstone, whose bright eyes had not missed the sorry condition of his two old friends, although he was naturally far too polite to refer to it directly, 'and I went off early one morning to make my fortune. Rather like your young Orinoco, I fancy. I believe I got about as far as Putney Bridge, when a policeman came up to me and asked what I was doing. Naturally I told him and the next thing I knew I was being marched off to the station house. In those days Human Beings were nervous about spies and enemy agents. I was questioned at great length and, of course, I had to stay silent a lot of the time otherwise . . .' and he shrugged.

'Quite, quite,' agreed Great Uncle Bulgaria.

'So they locked me up. It wasn't too difficult to get free. I had been working with Tobermory in the store and knew quite a lot about locks and keys. But I was now a hunted Womble and, I'll admit, panicky. Instead of making for Wimbledon I struck east and I eventually found myself in the dock areas. Some sailors were having a fight and soon the cops—er, policemen—came running up blowing their whistles. In my fear that it was me that they were after I took refuge on the first ship I came upon and there, quite exhausted, I went to sleep.'

'And woke up in America?' prompted Tobermory.

'No, indeed. In Lisbon, Portugal.'

'Dear me,' said Great Uncle Bulgaria, polishing his spectacles on his tartan shawl. 'And then?'

'I moved from ship to ship, always trying to get home and yet somehow managing to travel further and further away. I visited many places, Africa— which I may tell you is no place for Wombles as it's far too hot—then on again to India, where I met a most charming and cultivated Womble who had himself travelled down from the Khyber Pass. Did you know there was a Womble community there?'

'I had heard it talked of in my youth,' said Great Uncle Bulgaria, nodding.

'Is that right? This Womble's name was Quetta and we got on very well. I liked him and would have stayed, but by that time travel was in my blood. One thing he did tell me was that there were some snow-white Wombles, larger than us, up in the Himalayas in Tibet. Only there they go under a different name. Jeti or some such.'

'Really?' said Tobermory, who had just slipped back into the room after delivering Great Uncle Bulgaria's message to the two young Wombles. 'I didn't know that. Fascinating.'

'Then there was Melbourne, Australia. Christchurch, New Zealand—both have Womble communities who were most welcoming—and then I did the long Pacific haul and found myself in Canada . . .'

Cousin Yellowstone's voice died away and his eyes narrowed as he recalled those bitter months in the snows when he had so nearly died. He had run across traces of other Wombles, but they had all gone underground to sit out the winter, and so, slowly and painfully, he had made his way south to the United States. He shivered at the memory and then went on more cheerfully, 'And so I came to the States and it was there that I found a most flourishing community. They were very old-established and had travelled out shortly after the *Mayflower* and had settled down in Yellowstone Park. As you may recall that was the very name which I had always liked and had chosen for my own. It seemed such a good omen that I stayed. I meant it to be for just a short while, but time passes . . .'

'How very, very interesting,' said Great Uncle Bulgaria. 'And you make a good living?'

'Fantastic,' said Cousin Yellowstone. 'You would not believe just how much American Human Beings leave lying around. Why, do you know that nearly every Womble in the States could run a Cadillac if he so desired.'

Tobermory started slightly at this, but neither of the other two noticed it.

'However, most of us prefer to travel by paw. It's healthier and more independent. Yes, gentlemen, Womble-wise, the States is a *great* country. But enough of me and my affairs. I trust you didn't want this Orinoco to follow in my pawprints—at least not yet awhile?'

'Far too young and silly,' said Great Uncle Bulgaria. 'How did you come across him and Bungo?'

And so Cousin Yellowstone filled in his side of the story and Great Uncle Bulgaria and Tobermory listened and chuckled and said '*tsk, tsk*' and 'ho-hum' as the case might be.

'I trust you're not going to be too hard on him?' said Cousin Yellowstone finally.

'No, no, he's learnt his lesson,' said Great Uncle Bulgaria, 'and he appears to have brought back some food, which is useful. Things have been a little short with us recently.'

'If a loan would be of any help . . .' suggested Cousin Yellowstone, reaching for his wallet.

'No, no, wouldn't dream of it, thanks all the same,' said Great Uncle Bulgaria. 'Anyhow, what with Orinoco's two contributions and Bungo's and the thaw setting in at last we'll be all right again.'

'The trouble is, you see,' said Tobermory, scratching his ear with a screwdriver, 'we can't store sufficient quantities of food. There's plenty of it about in the warmer months, but we're unable to keep it for any length of time, apart from the bottled goods of course.'

'Is that right?' said Cousin Yellowstone. 'Well, a Womble with your brains should be able to solve the problem. What you need is a Deep Freeze.'

'A deep what?' said Tobermory, scratching

harder than ever.

'Freeze,' said Cousin Yellowstone. 'First thing tomorrow I'll try and explain how it works.'

'I suppose we couldn't start now?' said Tobermory hopefully.

'No, we could NOT,' snapped Great Uncle Bulgaria. 'I want to have a nice civilised talk. Now tell me, Yellowstone, do you remember the time in '12 or was it '13 that we had that perfectly splendid Midsummer party and . . .'

CHAPTER 12

GREAT UNCLE BULGARIA'S DAY OUT

As though to make up for the bad winter the spring was very mild and what with the soaking which the ground had received with the rains and the snow, followed by the warm weather, the Common bloomed and blossomed. The Queen's Mere melted and the fish reappeared apparently none the worse for having been deep frozen. The birds, those that had survived, started building nests in every available tree. Squirrels, badgers, rats, field mice, moles and, to everyone's surprise, a pair of otters, all came out of their winter quarters and wanted to know what all the fuss was about.

The Wombles, who once again were looking sleek, well cared for and plump, took no notice of these cheeky questions, as they had always followed a policy of ignoring lesser creatures, although in a perfectly polite way.

139

'Badgers are all right up to a point,' said Great Uncle Bulgaria, 'but slow. Got no conversation at all. And as for otters, well, they're as stupid as ducks and you can't get much sillier than *that*.'

'And squirrels,' said Tomsk, who had been doing his early morning exercises up in the trees and had had pawfuls of nuts thrown at him by the squirrels.

'Don't start mixing with that riff-raff,' said Great Uncle Bulgaria. 'Give them an inch and they'll take over a whole burrow before you can say Jack Womble; which reminds me, all ideas for the Midsummer outing must be put in the Suggestion Box by Friday at the latest.'

'I wish we could do something really tremendous this year,' said Bungo.

'I thought it was lovely last year,' said Alderney. 'Boats on Queen's Mere and coconut shies and a diving display.'

'The food was good too,' said Orinoco. He still wasn't *quite* his old fat self of pre-rabbit-hole-sticking days, but he looked very plump and well fed all the same. A strange change had come over his attitude to Bungo during the last few months. He no longer called him 'Young Womble', or 'Hi, you, Bungo', but treated him almost with respect, and Bungo in his turn had rather taken to hanging round Cousin Yellowstone, whom he admired enormously, for Bungo was never tired of hearing of his American relation's exciting world travels. One day perhaps he too would go off and see all those wonderful places.

'What would *you* like to do for the Midsummer outing?' he asked.

'Can't say I have many ideas on the subject,' said Cousin Yellowstone. 'Mind you, I remember the

140

days when I was about your age and I went to Wimbledon. My, that was great.'

'Wimbledon?' said Bungo, frowning. From what he had seen of it he didn't think it was anything so remarkable.

'Sure, the tennis tournament. I went just the once with my great-great-aunt Thessaly. It was quite an experience. We saw all the great players of the day. Yes, it was quite an occasion.'

'What were they doing?' Bungo whispered to Tomsk.

'Playing this game called tennis,' Tomsk whispered back. 'It's not as exciting as golf, but it's not bad in its way. I did the course in sixty-six yesterday, did I tell you?'

'About three hundred times,' said Bungo, but he spoke under his breath.

'At the first hole . . .' said Tomsk and he was off once again while Bungo nodded and said 'ho-hum' and 'tsk, tsk, tsk' without listening to one single word because his mind was on what Cousin Yellowstone had said. And so, as always, Bungo finally took his problem to Tobermory.

'Tickets for Wimbledon?' said Tobermory. 'Hold this vice for me, will you? Steady now. You might as well ask for gold dust. Haven't you seen the advertisements in *The Times* Personal Columns for them?'

'Perhaps if we wrote and asked to buy some, that way we might be lucky?' suggested Bungo, hanging on to the vice with all his strength while Tobermory hammered away at some mysterious piece of machinery.

'And where would you get the money? And what address would you put?' shouted Tobermory above the din.

Life was full of problems, thought Bungo. No sooner had you solved one than another sprang up to take its place. However, he was not a Womble to give up easily so he pinned a notice on the board by the main door saying that two tickets for Wimbledon were wanted urgently, and signed it 'Bungo Womble'. In the course of the next few days he was offered a single seat at the London Palladium, a return ticket to Bristol, and a season holder's pass for Lord's cricket ground.

'Cricket? That's kind of like baseball only slower, isn't it?' said Cousin Yellowstone, a remark which made Great Uncle Bulgaria's fur rise, until it occurred to him afterwards that in his young days Yellowstone had often watched cricket matches on the Common and that the American Womble was gently pulling their paws.

'Say, young Bungo,' Cousin Yellowstone said, 'about that question you were asking me; one summer a whole gang of my Wombles went to Coney Island for their party and it was a great success. Don't you have the same thing here on Hampstead Heath?'

'Yes, but it's too far,' said Bungo. 'Still, there's a Funfair in Battersea Park. That might be a good place for our outing. Only that'd be difficult to get to because the trains stop running quite early, I think. I'll check.' He was picking up a lot of American ways of speech.

'We could take cabs,' suggested Cousin Yellowstone, but this remark was not greeted with any degree of enthusiasm as, although the Wombles' reserves of money were swelling again, they were still not too healthy and Great Uncle

Bulgaria steadfastly refused to accept any kind of loan from his American relation.

'There must be a way to get these tennis ticket things,' said Bungo, setting his jaw. 'I do so want to give Cousin Yellowstone a really *good* present.' He still remembered with gratitude the way the American Womble had come to his rescue on the dark evening of the Great Adventure when he himself had been so desperate and felt so alone.

However, it wasn't Bungo who solved the problem, but Tomsk, who was now playing two rounds of golf a day. He set off one pearly dawn to put in some practice shots and was soon so engrossed in what he was doing that he failed to notice that a Human Being was following him round until he reached the last hole.

'Oh, good on you,' said this person, stepping over to Tomsk just as his ball trickled into the hole. 'My, that was a fair dinkum shot.'

'Thanks,' mumbled Tomsk.

'I haven't seen you out here before, have I?' went on the stranger, peering at Tomsk in some perplexity, as well he might since Tomsk was wearing Orinoco's straw hat, an enormous pair of dark glasses and a long red jacket. Tobermory, a stickler for doing things correctly, had insisted on this, as he had noticed that all the regular golfers (Human) wore red blazers.

'No, don't suppose so,' said Tomsk uneasily. He always tried to keep clear of Human Beings himself.

'You've got a marvellous follow-through,' went on the man, 'best I've seen since I left home. I'm an Australian, in case you haven't guessed that already.'

143

'No, I hadn't,' said Tomsk truthfully, only having the vaguest idea where Australia was.

'Too right I am. Over here for the tennis at Wimbledon. Suppose you wouldn't care to have a round with me? I'm not up to your class though; I'd better admit.'

'Tennis?' said Tomsk, dimly remembering some of Bungo's remarks. 'Yes, all right, I'll have a go, but I can't be too long. Got to get to work.'

'At this hour? It's only six o'clock,' said the Australian. 'OK then, sport. You tee off.'

Luckily Tomsk had been studying his golf manual throughout the winter so he knew what his opponent was talking about, although the Australian did appear a little startled when Tomsk said, 'Now I'm going to address you, ball,' and did.

It was really no match at all, for Tomsk had reduced his handicap and could now get round in sixty-three, an achievement which made the Australian say wonderingly, 'But you're amazing. You should take the game up professionally.'

'Can't,' muttered Tomsk, 'got a job already. I'm a Nightwatch Womble.'

'A what?'

'Sort of like a caretaker,' said Tomsk in an agony of embarrassment.

'Well, you're certainly a good golfer,' said the Australian. 'For such a small fellow your long shots are terrific. I can't say I like being beaten by you, but one thing I *do* know. I could knock the hide off you at tennis—I'm competing in the Wimbledon Championships.'

'Ho-hum,' said Tomsk.

'Would you like to see me play?' asked the Australian.

144

'Couldn't get in, no ticket,' said Tomsk, who was never a Womble for long speeches.

'Sure you could. I'll give you a double,' said the Australian, and took out two tickets and a card with his name on it and scribbled across the bottom. It was a very famous name in the tennis world, but Tomsk didn't know that.

'Well, so long, cobber, and thanks for the game.'

'Pleasure. Goodbye,' said Tomsk politely, and the moment the Australian was out of sight Tomsk went scampering back to the burrow, and was just in time to catch Bungo coming out to start his day's work.

'Got something to tell you,' said Tomsk.

'If it's about golf, *please* don't,' said Bungo.

'Well, 'tis and 'tisn't. Just thought you might be interested in a ticket for this Wimbledon thing. It *was* you who was asking about it, wasn't it?'

'What!' said Bungo, stopping in his tracks. 'Yes, it was. I say, Tomsk, old Womble, you're a genius.'

'Not really,' said Tomsk. He took a deep breath. 'It was like this. At the first hole I teed off and . . .'

'For me? Truly?' said Cousin Yellowstone, when Bungo rather shyly handed over the tickets and the card. 'Well, that's just marvellous. Just wait till I tell Great Uncle Bulgaria about this. He'll be thrilled.'

Great Uncle Bulgaria was not exactly thrilled, but he was extremely pleased, and he sent for Bungo and thanked him very much.

'Wasn't me really,' said Bungo. 'It was Tomsk who got the tickets, actually.'

'You're coming along, young Womble, coming along,' said Great Uncle Bulgaria and went hurrying off to see Madame Cholet about packing up a picnic tea for the great day. He also paid a visit to Tobermory's storeroom to choose a panama hat for himself, binoculars, and a very smart long white coat which only needed the arms shortening a trifle to fit perfectly.

'Can't let the side down, can we?' said Great Uncle Bulgaria, admiring his reflection in the hand mirror which Tobermory was holding up for him. 'And dark glasses I think. The glare's very bad on the Centre Court.'

'Fuss, fuss, fuss,' said Tobermory under his breath. To his way of thinking he had far more important matters on hand than going to see a lot of silly Human Beings running round a small piece of grass in pursuit of a ball. The truth of the matter was that Tobermory's nose had been put slightly out of joint ever since the arrival of Cousin Yellowstone. Nobody realised this, least of all Great Uncle Bulgaria, who had put his old friend's tetchiness down to whatever mysterious something he was up to in that back room of his.

As the Wimbledon Wombles had provided the tickets it was felt to be perfectly all right for Cousin Yellowstone to be responsible for the transport and, well hidden in the bushes, Bungo, Orinoco, Tomsk and Alderney watched them go off in a taxi.

'The burrow won't be the same without Great Uncle Bulgaria, will it?' said Alderney.

'Don't be silly, he's only gone for the afternoon. Race you home,' said Bungo. 'Besides I've got something I want to talk to you all about. One, two, three—GO!'

Tomsk won, of course.

Meanwhile Great Uncle Bulgaria and Cousin

Yellowstone were bowling up to the great Wimbledon stadium in fine style. It was a beautiful hot afternoon with a clear blue sky dotted with puffs of white clouds. Birds were singing everywhere and Human Beings in light coloured clothes were streaming into the grounds.

'What a sight,' breathed Great Uncle Bulgaria. 'Not bad, eh?'

'Very fine,' said Cousin Yellowstone, 'although Forest Hills is quite remarkable also.'

They climbed out of the taxi and Great Uncle Bulgaria was pleased and a little surprised, although he didn't show it, when the ticket collector on the gate bowed low and murmured something about the taxi being able to take them right inside if they so wished.

'No, no, we'll walk,' said Great Uncle Bulgaria, who was thoroughly enjoying looking at the colourful crowds strolling about. They were not, of course, as handsome as his Wombles, but as Human Beings go they weren't a bad-looking lot on the whole. Cousin Yellowstone too seemed impressed, although equally determined not to show it, and the two Wombles slowly made their way through the crowds to the ivy-covered walls of the great and famous Number One and Centre Courts.

It was here that they got their second surprise, for when Great Uncle Bulgaria produced their tickets and the card, the Human Being on the gate read the message on the card, saluted smartly and said, 'This way, sir, if you please, sir.'

A faint prickle of apprehension ran through Cousin Yellowstone's sleek grey fur. Were they by any terrible chance about to be led away for questioning as to how they had come by these rare tickets? He glanced at Great Uncle Bulgaria, whose face, what could be seen of it beneath the brim of his snowy white panama and the enormous round spectacles, was sunnily untroubled. Cousin Yellowstone braced himself.

'As the special players' stand is already full, gentlemen,' said the Human Being respectfully, 'alternative accommodation has been reserved. And as your tickets were given to you by . . .' and he named a very famous tennis player, 'I'm sure you two are the ones to whom it should be given. After you, sir.'

And to the astonishment of the two Wombles they were ushered through a very superior gateway.

'Why—surely—bless me—isn't this the way to the ROYAL box?' whispered Cousin Yellowstone.

'Naturally,' said Great Uncle Bulgaria without a quaver.

'Oh my,' said Cousin Yellowstone and mopped his face quickly with a silk handkerchief.

Slowly and as to the manner born Great Uncle Bulgaria allowed himself to be most respectfully ushered into a seat at the rear of the Royal box. With great dignity he sat down and clasped his paws over the head of his stick, staring steadfastly straight ahead at the emerald green court below. Not by a quiver of a whisker did he betray his own enormous surprise and satisfaction at this turn of events. All he did do was to kick his parcel of sandwiches gently under the seat, for Great Uncle Bulgaria knew, from reading the Court News in *The Times*, that persons who were invited to sit in the Royal box were also served with tea.

148

Cousin Yellowstone was even more impressed, but he kept his end up nobly, storing every incident in his mind to tell the Wombles back home in the States. He so far controlled himself as to comment adversely on the standard of modern tennis, which he said firmly was not nearly as good as when he was a young Womble.

'It's all in the service these days,' he said. 'If *that*'s powerful enough you're almost sure to win.'

'What energy they have,' said Great Uncle Bulgaria, watching the players leap about the court untiringly. 'Oh, well played, sir!' And he clapped his paws enthusiastically.

They were lucky enough to have been given their seats for the Saturday of the first week, so that the tennis they were watching was of an extremely high standard without being too nerve-racking. Great Uncle Bulgaria enjoyed every second of it, and it wasn't until the shadows slowly drew across the court that he was able to turn his attention from the tennis to those sitting in front of him.

'So like her great-great-grandmother,' he sighed, looking at the beautiful Royal Person sitting at the front of the box. 'That smile, that way she has of lifting her hand. Ah me, how it takes me back.'

However, even all the excitement and the colour and the applause did not stop Great Uncle Bulgaria hooking up his sandwiches at the finish— they *were* given tea in a private lounge—because for the life of him Great Uncle Bulgaria could never, under *any* circumstances, be untidy.

'That was great, just great,' said Cousin Yellowstone, letting out a loud sigh of appreciation. 'Just wait until I tell the Wombles back home about it. And sitting in the same section as Her.'

'So you intend to leave us,' said Great Uncle Bulgaria.

'I have to go back, yes,' said Cousin Yellowstone as they slowly made their way down the stairs. 'I have business interests and so forth which must be attended to, and our annual Womble Conference comes up later in the Fall. It is a very, very important occasion.'

'We shall miss you,' said Great Uncle Bulgaria. 'You've done so much for us with your ideas on the Deep Freeze system, and your Efficiency Scheme.'

'It's all been a pleasure. And hospitality-wise you have all been more than kind. I only wish I could show my deep gratitude in some more personal way,' replied Cousin Yellowstone, who was not to be outdone in the business of being polite.

'Well, there is just one little thing,' said Great Uncle Bulgaria, seeing his chance and taking it with both paws. 'Knowing the scope of your organisation—er—Womble-wise—would it be possible for you to trace a Human Being for us? His name is Donald Smith and he went to live in Butte, Montana, some twenty years ago. His father is now elderly and, I'm afraid, very poor and lonely. He would very much like to re-establish contact with his son. I could give you the old gentleman's address in Wimbledon . . . but perhaps it is too difficult a task?'

'It shall be done. I shall see to it personally,' said Cousin Yellowstone. 'Discreetly, of course; our Wombles in Public Relations work to keep our name out of the news.'

'Splendid, splendid,' said Great Uncle Bulgaria. 'Dear me, what is going on?'

For the people in front of them had stopped and were all bunching together.

'I can't quite make out,' said Cousin Yellowstone. 'Oh yes, I see, it's the Royal car. It's just leaving and the photographers are taking pictures.'

Slowly the people moved on again, but the cameramen's flashbulbs continued to explode and as at the very end of the procession Great Uncle Bulgaria and Cousin Yellowstone descended the steps the photographers took their final pictures.

'What a day to remember this has been,' said Cousin Yellowstone as they drove away in a taxi. 'Yes, sir. I just wish I had some little memento to show my Wombles back home.'

And oddly enough his wish was granted, for two days later an elderly lady happened to leave her copy of *The Times* behind on the Common and when Bungo picked it up and took it to the burrow, there on the sports page was a photograph of Great Uncle Bulgaria and Cousin Yellowstone on the steps of the Royal entrance and underneath was the caption: *Distinguished Visitors leave Wimbledon Tennis Tournament*.

'Quite right too,' said Great Uncle Bulgaria, and cut it out and signed it, and Tobermory—whose temper was now back to normal—framed it and they had a little party of old Wombles, at which Great Uncle Bulgaria made a speech and presented the picture to Cousin Yellowstone to show 'the Wombles back home'.

CHAPTER 13

TOBERMORY'S SURPRISE AND THE MIDSUMMER PARTY

It was while all this was going on that Bungo put his idea for the Midsummer party into the Suggestion Box. It was such a very unusual idea that he had little hope of its being accepted and very nearly forgot all about it until Tobermory sent for him.

'If it's about that puncture kit I found, it was on my piece of ground, honestly,' said Bungo anxiously.

'I believe you,' said Tobermory. 'No, it's not about that, nor the Thermos flask, nor that very good camera.'

'Aren't Human Beings strange?' said Bungo, leaning on the work bench.

'Extraordinary,' agreed Tobermory. 'I've seen them come and I've seen them go more years than

152

I care to remember, but I'll *never* understand them. However, young Bungo, it's not about any of those things I want to see you. It's your suggestion for the Midsummer party I'm interested in.'

'Oh, that,' said Bungo. 'Well, you see it sort of came to me that it might be fun to go to Battersea Funfair. I suppose it's impossible though. How could we all get there?'

'Exactly,' said Tobermory. 'Well, it may surprise you to know, young Bungo, that some of your seniors aren't quite as out of date as you may think. Come with me. And you, Orinoco, and Tomsk and Alderney.' For they were all hanging about in the doorway of the Workshop. Bungo had become their leader and they followed him everywhere.

And Tobermory led them through the maze of small storerooms until he reached the last room of all, and then he stood aside and said, 'There', in a very proud voice. And he had every reason for his pride, for standing in the centre of the workroom was a small bus, or a large car—depending on your point of view.

Tobermory had been working on it in every spare moment for the last eight months and although no car manufacturer would have been able to say with absolute certainty that it was one of his models, it was still, undoubtedly, a vehicle. A vehicle of very mixed pedigree, perhaps but a vehicle.

'Gosh,' said Bungo. 'Gosh. I say—does it go?'

'It does,' said Tobermory, stroking the bonnet. 'I've been saving every drop of concentrated nettle and acorn juice for weeks and weeks. This morning I started her up. Watch.' And he climbed into the driving seat and switched on and the car-bus roared into life so loudly that Alderney dived behind Bungo for protection.

'You are clever,' she said.

'It's very fine,' said Orinoco.

'I bet it goes fast,' said Tomsk.

'I expect it *will*,' said Tobermory, switching off and climbing down. 'Now then, off with the lot of you. I'm expecting Great Uncle Bulgaria.'

Of course it wasn't as simple as all that, for the car-bus, which was christened the Silver Womble by an almost unanimous vote, was imprisoned, so to speak, in the burrow. Tobermory drew up some plans for a special tunnel to be built (and reinforced with concrete), and himself made two large doors, cleverly camouflaged, which were just wide enough to let the Silver Womble out on to the Common. Also Tobermory wasn't too sure about his driving, so he sat up reading *The Car Driver's Handbook, The Driving Test and You, What Every Motorist Should Know* and *Simple Mechanics* night after night, and at the end of a week he very cautiously took the Silver Womble out for her first road trials.

Bungo pleaded to go with him and the two of them rumbled round and round the Common (luckily there was no moon) until even Tobermory was satisfied that he had got the hang of driving.

The other Wombles too were hard at work. Madame Cholet insisted that every young Womble had to help her with the food. Great Uncle Bulgaria made out the final timetables and programmes, which all had to be copied out for the heads of departments. Tomsk was kept on the run carrying parcels of food, tins of the concentrated nettle and acorn juice and messages, and Orinoco gave up all hope of snatching a nice forty winks, because Great Uncle Bulgaria had made him his Private Office Womble. He made a little round badge with POW on it, hung it on a string round his neck and trotted up and down the burrow feeling very important.

'Gives him a feeling of responsibility. Takes his mind off his stomach too,' said Great Uncle Bulgaria.

In fact, the week before the outing was extremely active for everyone and Wombles of every shape and size and age, even the very small ones, scurried in all directions and in the course of this activity the Common was scoured as never before. It only needed a careless picnicker to drop a drinking carton and there was a Womble behind the nearest bush to pick it up. Or a bad-tempered child to throw away a chocolate biscuit and a Womble would swoop on it. Or an old lady to leave a bag of peppermints on a bench and a Womble would whisk it off. For as Great Uncle Bulgaria so rightly said, 'Every little helps.'

All kinds of wonderful things piled up in Tobermory's Workshop and he hummed and said, '*tsk, tsk, tsk*' and sorted them out before you could say Jack Womble. In fact, since Cousin Yellowstone had announced that he must definitely leave for the States on July the first, Tobermory had grown increasingly cheerful.

'It's all go,' panted Orinoco, setting off on his bicycle, to which Tobermory had fitted an enormous basket. He had also made Orinoco a long stick with a spike on the end of it (similar to those carried by the Common Keepers) and

Orinoco fairly whizzed about tidying up his patch.

Great Uncle Bulgaria tapped his barometer and the needle stayed firmly at high. Alderney pushed her trolley up and down the passages with the bell tinkling non-stop, Madame Cholet cooked and planned and stored exciting-looking packets away in the Deep Freeze, and Tomsk actually stopped playing golf for a week and volunteered to do some tidying up in his spare time. As for Bungo, he was here, there and everywhere, beside himself with excitement. And in the middle of it all was Great Uncle Bulgaria making plans at his own efficient, calm pace, but just as excited as everybody else although he didn't show it.

And so at last the great day dawned, with every Womble hard at work as soon as the sun rose. They had breakfast at eight and worked inside the burrow after that, as there were a great many Human Beings about because of the warm weather. Lunch, a not very big meal, was served at one, and there were a few more jobs to do, and then at three, sharp bells rang up and down the passages and all the Wombles, Great Uncle Bulgaria included, went to their beds and slept, or tried to. At ten the bells were rung again, and up and down the burrow Wombles stirred and brushed themselves and cleaned their teeth and looked at their excited reflections in mirrors. For the Midsummer party is the biggest, most important and happiest occasion of the year.

At ten o'clock they all lined up outside the kitchen where Madame Cholet, wearing a flowered apron, was doling out their party food. By ten thirty, with eyes shining and fur gleaming, they were lining up by the main door, where Tomsk, looking very important, was on duty with a list of names. At ten forty-five there was a rumbling noise and Tobermory, wearing a flat cap, goggles and a long coat, appeared at the wheel of the Silver Womble which bore the number plate:

WOM I

He was shaking with excitement, but his face was dignified and grave as he picked up his first passengers: Great Uncle Bulgaria, Madame Cholet—now wearing a hat with flowers on it and a feather boa—Cousin Yellowstone, Bungo, Orinoco, Alderney and twenty-four of the youngest Wombles.

Slowly and very carefully the Silver Womble moved across Wimbledon Common beneath the golden light of the rising moon. Tobermory, who was always very thorough, had taken the time and trouble to study all the latest road maps, so he completed the journey to Battersea Park without a hitch, dropping his party at the gates at exactly midnight.

'Isn't it beautiful?' said Alderney.

'Not as good as Wimbledon though,' said Bungo, and Alderney hung on to his arm and nodded violently.

'Quite pleasant,' said Madame Cholet, shaking out her boa.

'Allow me,' said Great Uncle Bulgaria, offering her his arm.

By one o'clock every single Wimbledon Womble—and Cousin Yellowstone of course—was in Battersea Park. They strolled about and had a look at the River Thames, which had turned to silver in the moonlight, and admired the flower beds and the lake and the tennis courts. The deer looked rather startled, but soon went back to sleep again and one or two rabbits and a few squirrels came out to see what was going on, but the Wombles, naturally, ignored them.

And so, at last, it was time to enter the Funfair itself. It was quite deserted and all the lights were switched off, but that did not deter the Wombles in the least. They swarmed over everything. Bungo had a go down the water chute and Orinoco went sliding after him.

'What price Queen's Mere?' said Bungo, as they both came up dripping wet.

'Dalmatian dogs to you,' said Orinoco, and went under again as Bungo, spluttering and laughing, pushed his head beneath the water.

Tomsk had a go at the punchballs and was quite

convinced that he would have won a prize. Madame Cholet inspected the snack bars, the restaurant and the kiosk where they made candy floss, and said with quiet pride that her cooking would undoubtedly stand the comparison between what they produced and what she provided.

Great Uncle Bulgaria had a look at absolutely everything and was particularly interested in the slot machines.

'Surely you could work out a system to win on these things?' he said to Tobermory.

'I expect so,' agreed Tobermory, whose mind was on other matters. 'Excuse me,' and he hurried off to inspect the Big Dipper. He soon realised that it would be quite impossible to set the little cars in motion as that would wake the inhabitants of Battersea, but surely a Womble might be able to manage without a car at all?

'I wonder now,' said Tobermory, and hoisted himself on to the track and gave himself a gentle push off; and that, naturally enough, did it, and the next moment Tobermory was shooting down the slide with increasing speed. It was a wonderful sensation, so wonderful that he nearly came right off at the first bend, but luckily instinct came to his rescue and he navigated it successfully and went careering off on the next dizzy drop downwards. And after that every Womble, except Great Uncle Bulgaria and Madame Cholet, just had to have a go, even Cousin Yellowstone, and for the next two hours the Big Dipper was covered in Wombles sliding and slipping and slithering for all they were worth. Some sitting down, some standing up, and some doing it the daring way on their round stomachs.

By the time they were all thoroughly exhausted, Madame Cholet had collected up all their parcels of food and had arranged them beside the boating pool, and as every Womble was ravenously hungry they sat down and ate and ate and ate until even Orinoco couldn't manage one crumb more.

It was indeed, as even the older Wombles agreed, the very best Midsummer party they had ever enjoyed. Perhaps the terrible winter which they had been through made them all, even the smallest, appreciate this golden Midsummer's Eve more than usual. But be that as it may, as they sat round the pool which reflected the stars and the now slowly sinking yellow moon, they were all very happy and extremely contented.

'It's been a jolly good party,' said Tomsk.

'Lovely,' agreed Alderney.

'Grub was good,' said Orinoco.

'Wasn't that slide fun?' said Bungo, hiding a yawn.

'Time to go home,' said Great Uncle Bulgaria, who had seen the first faint streaks of pink dawn showing in the eastern sky. Sleepily and slowly the Wombles collected everything up and stuffed their paper bags into the wastebins. There wasn't any food left to collect. And then one by one, yawning and stretching, they lined up to be driven back to Wimbledon Common.

Bungo was one of the last to leave and as they travelled through the rapidly lightening streets he thought sleepily about the last year. About the Dalmatian dog and the first day's work on the Common and Orinoco and the big black umbrella. About the dreadful rain and the even more frightening snow and the great famine and the affair of the snow Womble. About Orinoco running away and the finding of Cousin Yellowstone, and Tomsk and the toppling tree and his passion for golf. About the Deep Freeze and Tobermory's Silver Womble, and last of all about the wonderful party and Great Uncle Bulgaria getting his picture in *The Times*.

What a lot had happened and what a very *young* Womble he had been when he first started work.

'Home,' said Tobermory's voice in Bungo's ear, and he scrambled out more asleep than awake and stood blinking in the rose-coloured dawn. The Common looked very beautiful and rather mysterious in this fragile pink light and Bungo blinked at it and rubbed his paws in his eyes while the other Wombles walked past him whispering and laughing as they made for their beds.

'Well, young Womble,' said Great Uncle Bulgaria, coming up behind Bungo. 'Enjoy yourself, eh?'

'Oh *yes*,' said Bungo fervently.

'Good.'

Great Uncle Bulgaria put one snow-white paw on his shoulder and for a time both of them watched the pink light stretching across the grass and making the shadows grow shorter and shorter. In the distance the roar and rumble of the never-ending traffic was growing louder and an airliner hummed overhead with its landing lights flashing.

'It's a funny sort of world,' said Great Uncle Bulgaria, pulling his tartan shawl more closely round his shoulders, for although it was going to be another hot day there is always a sudden cool wind that springs up at dawn.

He turned to look at the young Womble at his

161

side.

'Bungo,' said Great Uncle Bulgaria musingly. 'Bungo—not a *bad* sort of name really. Quite *sensible*, in fact. Give me your arm.'

And side by side the two of them went down into the burrow and Tomsk shut and bolted the door behind them and ticked the last names off his list, and went yawning and stretching off his to bed. Outside the sun came up as red as a new penny over the horizon and turned the grass of Wimbledon Common to gold for a few fleeting moments. But not a single Womble was there to see, for as Orinoco said afterwards, 'They were all having a nice *eighty* winks.'